T0208831

GOD'S PATH

TO SPIRITUAL ENLIGHTENMENT
SECOND EDITION

NAOLA KAYLANI DAVIS

authorHOUSE®

AuthorHouse™
1663 Liberty Drive
Bloomington, IN 47403
www.authorhouse.com
Phone: 1 (800) 839-8640

Published by AuthorHouse 07/26/2019

ISBN: 978-1-7283-0047-4 (sc)
ISBN: 978-1-7283-0045-0 (hc)
ISBN: 978-1-7283-0046-7 (e)

Library of Congress Control Number: 2019901805

Print information available on the last page.

Cover photograph by Naola Davis

2nd Edition Table of Contents

My God

06/02/2014

My God is a good God,
My God is a good God,
My God is a good God
Oh yes he is.
Yes he is.

My God is a good God,
My God is a good God,
My God is a good God
Oh yes he is.
Yes he is.

My God takes my burdens
My God takes my cares
My God loves me,
When nobodies there.
My God loves me
When nobody cares.

My God knows what to do
My God knows when and where.
My God
My God, only God

He is my strength
When I am weak,
He is there.

He is my joy,
When I am down
He brings me laughter
In the midst of sorrow.

He is my everything,
My God is my
All in a weary land.

My God is a good God,
My God is a good God,
My God is a good God.
Oh yes he is.
Oh yes he is

I Long for You

11/04/2015

My heart longs for you,
my soul longs for you,
my body longs for you.
There is a completeness;
that will take place.

When my soul's craving
Is complete,
not until that time,
will my soul's craving cease.

What does it mean
to long for the one
who touches your spirit
and touches your soul?

There is an emptiness,
a hollow place in your
heart that needs to be
filled for the longing to
cease the pain.
I long for you,
every day,
and every hour,
I long for you.

My longing is more
than just a hope,
more than just a desire,
it is an emotion that,
brings me joy at its completeness,
sorrow as I long for what,
I know is.

I long for you,
my heart aches with desire.
It aches with the
Loneliness without you.

I long for you.
I long for you.
I always have,
longed for you.

Nothing

11/04/2015

No nothing, no nothing
Will ever stop
the feelings I have
for you.

Nothing, not death,
Nothing can stop
The vibrations I
feel from you.

Even after death,
the vibrations
exist.
The loved one is,
Still loved.

As long as,
the loved one is
still loved,
nothing can stop
the vibrations of love.

There is no way,
to diminish love's vibration,
love is a vibration,
which exists on,
many planes.

Love's vibrations can
be seen and felt on
Many levels.

When a parent
looks at a child,
the emotion of pure,
joy and delight create
a vibration between the
parent and child,
which exists after death.

The beauty that fills the earth,
Flowers, animals and the beauty of buildings,
parks and oceans,
are a love, that
can not be diminished.

Our love is strong.
There are bonds,
That no chains,
No separation can
Break.

Nothing, no not
Anything can break
The bonds of love.

Love is a
Vibration which
Is as essential,
as breathing.
It is life,

It is the core
of human beings.

Love is the life
force, which continues
Even after death,
It is the beauty
Of what is most,
enjoyed.

Love, will never be stopped,
No not anything,
Nothing will stop love.
The creator in his
Wisdom created a life
force within each and
everyone of us
that can not be stopped.

It is invisible,
but can be felt,
Once felt,
It is a magnetic force that
Draws the heart in for
Complete fulfillment.

The heart desires
More, it can never,
Get enough of
The joy of love.
Nothing,
Can prevent the

Invisible force of nature (God)
From its joy.

Love can, be seen,
In all the wonders
Of this earth.
Love, love, love
Nothing can stop love.

Matthew 5-8

8/15/2015

"Blessed are the pure in heart for they shall see God"

Today Ventura College laid to rest an
outstanding history professor
of over 40 years tenure. He was a good soul who did all he could
for students, his community while fighting for Civil Rights.

I just couldn't go
I could not witness
His still body,
He was so vibrant in my mind.

Mayo was pure in heart,
He had a generous out going
giving heart.
Whatever he could,
do to help others
is what he did.

I just could not
Go, I was one of his student's
He taught and gave to his students,
as all teachers should.

I just could not go,
My memories of him

The giving vibrant
Alive man
will remain intact.

I just could not go,
Mayo has enhanced Ventura
College on so many occasions
By the classes he taught,
While striving for equal rights for all.

I just wanted his
Memory to be that of
A smiling gregarious teacher,
Who lent a hand to help all who struggle.

It did not matter your color
It did not matter your race or gender
He supported all who had a need,
The epitome of a pure heart.

Today Mayo's fight
Will be carried on by others
Enfolded into the arms of
The almighty.

There are so many
Stars in his crown
The almighty says,
"Well done my son,
Well done."

1/16/2016

I miss you very much. I think of you
often our encounter has been
brief but left a lasting memory. When I think of you. I smile for
no apparent reason.

My thoughts are of when I will see you. I am watching
"Sleepless in Seattle" which makes me desire the next time we
will meet even more. I am beginning to wonder if, but then I am
determined to have faith.

There is so much, I don't know about you, like sports, which
ones you like. I think you are into coaching, perhaps football,
baseball, basketball, soccer. Tennis.

I never thought it would come to this, that our feelings would
be what they are. I thank God for you we have to fight for us.

Be blessed,
Naola

You Make My Heart Sing

3/7/2013

You make my heart sing,
You make my heart sing,
You make my heart sing,
You make my heart leap
For joy.

Just you, just you
Can do what no
Others can do
Just you, just you, just you,
Turn my heart into jello,
just you melt away my fears,
you melt away my cares...
Being with you makes me feel a love
No others can do.

Just you, just you, just you.
All I want to do is be with you.
All I want to do is
Be with you.

You are mine
And I am yours,
All I want to do is be with you.
All I want to do is be with you.

You are mine,
And I am yours,
All I want to do is be with you.

I want the world to know
That you are true,
And what I feel for you is real.
I want the world to know
What I feel for you is real,
I want the world to know what I feel
For you is real.

I have looked my whole life for you,
I have looked my whole life for you,
And now I have found you,
And now I have found you,
And you have found me,
No other will do,
We are one,
We are one.

No mountains,
No oceans,
No rivers,
No valleys
No deserts,
No nothing will stand between us.
Our love reaches
Higher than mountains,
Deeper than the ocean and valleys,
Wider than deserts.

Nothing, no nothing,
Will separate us.
Nothing, no nothing
Will separate us.

I am yours,
And you are mine
From the dawn of time,
Forever, forever, and forever more.

For you make my heart sing.
The joy we feel is real
For you make my heart sing.

Are You Thinking About Me?

9/29/2013

I am close to God
Always
When there is no reason
No cause
I think of you
The combination of two
Is what the father says
Let no man put asunder.

Two shall be one
No longer two
But the one that the
Souls create
During the symbiotic
Joining of mind, body, heart and soul.

Spirits search endlessly for
the one who can
make them think about
The other that
Is really not the other
but a part of the
Whole that split and
Became one then became
Two, the joining to become
One and a part of the whole again.

It is amazing that
What appears to be one
and solitary, has never
really been just one,
has always been
A part of the whole.

The souls magnetic attraction
May not realize they have
Found their other half
When they look at
the other with their eyes alone

But one touch,
One electrifying stroke
Of the hand on the others
Arm and the electrical charge
Given off makes it
Difficult to remain as one
With the spiritual knowledge
That this is a connection
That will never be parted.

The desire to become one
Is so strong that the
Sprit melds with the other
and a love never known
Is and was
it is just a bloom
but it reaches for the energy
That fulfills its completeness.

Are you thinking of me?
Is that why I am thinking
Of you?
My need for my other half
gets more intense as the sands
Of time run down.

I wish I could stop
Time when we are together,
and feel this connection.
The only way this can be
is when the father
Breathes is voice into the vibrations
That is now and forever
Will be one.

Our Souls Meet

03/21/2015

Once again
our souls meet
in this place at
this time.

Once again
our souls meet
we connect on the
astral highway.

Like ships passing
in the night
dancing, twriling
and passing other
souls by.

Our souls meet
we could have kept
traveling but our souls
connection through a glance,
a chance encounter.

Our souls stopped
we thought to take a
brief indulgence
our souls meet once
again our souls meet.

Our souls density
and fusion connect
in a way that is
not easily forgotten.

Our souls intertwining
With one another
instead of two
there becomes one.

Like the intertwining of
fingers, yours and mine
become one,
in that brief second
we become one
for a fleeting moment.
We become inexplicably
Touched to the core
while the world glances
in startled amazement.

The amazement is not theirs
alone, it is ours
To reflect upon
and wonder what happened?

Once again our souls
meet, once again
we stop and hesitate,
do we dare linger.

Or once again
should we travel
on the celestial highway,
as joyous,
because once again
our souls meet.

Can That Someone Be you?

1/30/2015

Can you be someone
From a distant past?
Because thoughts of you
take my breath away.

Thoughts of you create
a physical energy
a mental longing just
to be near you again.

Logically this makes no
sense to feel so close
so soon because thoughts
of you set up a longing in me
of what could be
a longing of remembering
perhaps that which once was
in our past that is
hard to grasp.

Thoughts of you
enter my mind once too often,
at times I can barely
catch my breath because
the longing can be uncomfortable
the longing brings images to mind
that my soul longs to become more.

Once I saw you
I could not forget you.
Months passed and you
were filtering, moving
in and out of my mind
the celestial space that
holds you captive in my mind and heart.

Your connection to me
though impossible creates
a force that plays tag with you
on this side
stimulating my longing for
you even more than you
could possibly know.

I long to be touched by you
To be held by you
kissed by you.
It would stimulate
the distant memories I feel
I know you.

Thoughts of you make my
heart sing so I catch my
breath because I feel you
Thoughts of you create a
knowing and understanding
of the you, you once were,
I feel you so deeply it
tears at my heart

it tears at my spirit
it tears at my soul.

When I see you
I can barely look at you
when I see you
thoughts of you and what we
once were tear at my mind.
I can barely look at you
for fear you will discover
the secrets your presence brings to bare.

Thoughts of you and
Something in the past we
Could have shared
It is immobilizing but my
Heart and mind ask if it could be?
Is our secret mystery
held in the distant past?

Why do thoughts of you
make my toes curl?
Brings a smile to my
Lips, and the connection
I feel to you brings a joy
So deep and satisfying
It is hard to fathom,
Why?

We Touched

6/13/2017

It was an accident
but not
touch is
more than a touch.

Because if it were not
would you give it
more than a moments
pause.

I paused
I wondered if it would
ever take place,
spontaneous, brief and quick.

It was the first touch,
not to be forgotten
the first touch,
I wonder,
did he give it a pause?

I wonder if
he has already forgotten
that moment,
that brief interlude,
maybe, but maybe not.

I think on it

and a smile radiates
from my heart.

You can't say
it was accidental
but a moment where
in spontaneity
our hands, no fingers caught
hold for one brief moment.

I thought, we touched
it was so spontaneous
it was so natural,
as if we had been friends
for a while, and afterwards
I thought, with a smile
we touched.

We touched in that
moment that I needed him
to reassure me
we touched in that moment
while he assured me
we touched.

It was brief
But the moments
that follow
will last a life time
because we touched.

You Are My Angel

01/01/2014

I believe in you,
You have stood by me
For a time

You have sent
Those to help and care
For me
I believe in you.

You are the unknown
Angel that only I know
That it is you.

You help me when you
Are angry with me
Your love for me
Knows no physical limitations,
As does mine for you.

I believe in you
I have faith in you
I love you today and tomorrow
In addition tomorrows, tomorrow.

You are the Angel in
My life.
You watch over me
And protect me

From that which would
Do harm.

The Angel of my life
You know what takes
Place in my life.
I trust you
You are my Angel.

You are my Angel
You are my Angel
You take care of me
What can I say?

How do I thank my Angel?
The depth and magnitude of
My gratitude shine
A dim light to the depth of my thanks.

You are my angel
You are my angel
And I love you so.

Skies Are Blue

And Baby
I Love You

12/31/2013

The seas are blue
And baby
I love you.

You are the epitome
Of what I want in a man
But sadly
You are too far
On a distant horizon

I love so many things
About you and the way
You love others too.

You are red and
Daffodils are white
The skies are cloudy
But what really matters is that
I love you.

Love is interesting
You try to place it on another
But the soul's electricity
Must ignite the others.

I love you but
You are too far
And all I can do is
Dream of you.

The seas are blue
And the skies are blue
But baby I still love you.

When I think of you
I feel your presence
Although you are not here
And at times
I know that you feel me too
For our love is deep and compromising.

The knowledge that
No matter the circumstance
We love each other
Deeply and completely.

This knowledge is spiritual
And relayed by the
Omnipotent,
That only we know what we know
About our love.

How this happened
It does not matter
The deep and searing love
I feel for you, you may never know
Because you will never
Get this love letter.

I tell myself to move on
And find another
It is almost impossible to do.

So sweetheart if I should
Pass before you
I hope this poem finds you,
And you will realize that
I loved you totally and
Completely
As one in love should do.

The Skies are blue
Seas are blue
And baby, I Love you.

The One I Need

1/19/2014

The man I need
showers me with millions
of little kisses
from my head to my feet.

The one I need
Caresses my shoulders
with the warmth of
his hands and his mouth.

His tongue is gentle
and rough at the same time
as he ignites the
fires of my desire
underneath.

He is strong and gentle
at the same time.
His touch is a warm
breeze as a humid
summer night.

His touch stirs the
passions that lay dormant
inside of me.
It is like the fire that strokes the powder keg
which is explosive.

His touch ignites
all that desire that
lays dormant
inside of me.

His touch quickens
my very soul,
the strokes of his hands
and tongue drive me
to a passion that is
like a delirious frenzy
that drives me
to the height of ecstasy
and pleasure.

I want him to stop before
I reach the break
but I don't want him to continue
but I do need him to continue.

I am delirious
with his touch.
I am filled in my heart
with emotion that touches
my soul and reaches
the regions that can only
be satisfied with his entirety.

It makes me move
from side to side
Up and down
in and out.
Ignited by the passion

of his kisses
and his tongue.

I want. I need him
to stop but I don't
I want this delirium
to last forever if it can.

But that is not possible
it is only a moment
in time when
the two become one
our souls touch and join
because of the passion and
ecstasy ignited by his kiss and
his touch.

When two become one
the physical ignites
the spiritual
and the spiritual ignites
the physical
because it is so deep
it is difficult to come
up for air, because it
continues to explore and deepen
the passion it began.

The one I need does
this for me
and I for him.
One look can start it
one look and the desire

for him to touch my
soul and spirit is there.

The one I need
needs me too.
He knows I am here
but too afraid of such
a deep blissful passion.

The one I need
needs me too,
The one I need
needs me too.

It is a Mystery to Me

09/25/2013

It is a mystery
To me why I love you
It is much too soon
To feel this way for you

It is a mystery to me
Why I feel this way for you
It is a puzzle that
I cannot piece together

It is a mystery to me
Why I feel this love for you
It is much too soon
To feel these emotions
It is a puzzle that
Only God above can solve

It is a mystery to me
Why I keep thinking about you
Why thoughts of our last
Moments together
Are still vivid on my mind
Making love to you
Is all that it is supposed to be

It is a mystery to me
Why I long to kiss you

And be kissed by you
I can still feel your
Lips on me and the searing
Pleasure your lips
Bring to mine

It is a mystery to me
How our paths crossed
Not once, but twice
And that knowledge makes
Me think that God with
His omnipotent power was
Moving us closer and closer
Through time and space

It is a mystery to me
How God created the universe
And in this universe, through
its mass of time and space
Two souls can find its other half

God moves, creates and shapes
That which we see
That which we are
And that which we will be

We search our entire
Lives for the completeness
That we feel with our
Other half, the satisfaction
We find knows no bounds

For time and space are limitless
To these souls who have
Been brought together

It is a mystery to me
The love that we share
That knows no bounds
Of time and space
Our love knows no bounds
Our love knows no bounds
It is a mystery to me
It is a mystery to me...

I Have Never Met You

I have never met you
But I have dreamed
Of you
When we talked
I really did not know
Who you were
I thought, nice man
And a pleasant possibility

When you first begin a
Conversation, you really
Want that person
To be the one
So I began to dream that
You could possibly be the one

The one who could make my
Heart beat faster
The one who I would want
To share all my dreams
Mundane or not
The one who could just
Turn me on by the sound
Of your voice
The one I have always
Dreamed of

We have never met
But we have a relationship

We have never met but
I know you are there
We have never met
But I can feel you
Deep, deep, down
In my soul

I have loved you
From a far for years
For longer than is possible
Longer than reality
You are my dream
And in reality
I love you from a far

We have never met
But I have dreamed
Of you
I have desired you
And wondered what it would
Feel like to be held by you
And for our legs to intertwine

I dream of you
Your picture is available
But this is not reality
Just a dream I have of you

You are the man of my
Dreams that I hope
Someday to meet
You have touched my
Soul by just being you

You are the man
Of my dreams
Don't give up,
Don't let go I
Will be there with you
Soon, not just in my
Dreams, the universe has
A way of making our dreams
Come true, as it will
For me and you

I have never met you
But I have dreamed
Of you

The Blanket of Your Warmth

I receive your warmth,
It is a blanket that
Protects me from the cold,
That generates heat,
The blanket warms my heart
And quickens my soul and my spirit

The warmth stimulates
My neither regions
And makes me desire
To look at you, your face and your eyes
Which are the
Entrance to your soul

I am motivated to dance
And sing to the pure
Joy and fulfillment this
Warmth brings me

Am I alone in this joy?
Are we not one in this
Heart's warmth fulfillment?
The pull of the joy is so
Strong that my heart is
Contrite and pains of
The knowledge that our
Connection has made
Us long for completion

I now have this need
Which was not there
Your warmth covered
Me and contracted my heart

Am I alone in this
Or do you feel it too
When you talk of me
Do your long to be with me
And look into my eyes
For the soul's completion

Do you tingle in your
Neither regions because the
Excitement that thoughts of me
Bring to you
Never ceasing because we are
Also thinking of each other
At the same time
Never ceasing
Never ceasing

My heart though constricted
Beats too fast when
The blanket of your warmth
Heats my body and shields
My heart and a slow
But bright glow forms
Because your blanket of
Warmth surrounds me

I muse as I look at
The leaves on trees

Dancing in the wind
And I watch the sunlight dancing
On the leaves making the
Leaves glisten while they dance
To the melody of the breeze

And yet I feel I need you,
because the connection
Is strong, once experienced
Hard to forget
The blanket of your warmth
Surrounds me and won't let
Me forget, the need for you
It creates in me.

The blanket of your warmth
Always surrounding me
Won't let me forget the need
You create in me.

The blanket of your warmth
Has created a cocoon
That wraps us both, which
Only heaven and God
Could create
For the power is God's to
Join man and woman and
Create a glorious union
On earth and heaven

The blanket of your warmth
Satisfies me

As nothing else can
Made by God and heaven above

I don't fear
I know it is real
The blanket of your warmth
Created from God above
The Blanket of your warmth.

Soulmates

10-27-2018

Originally, I thought a person could only have one soul mate
throughout their life journey. I have found in my estimation that
this is not the case. If you are lucky,
enough to find one soul mate
then another this makes for complexities
in life. First of all the soul
mate is the soul's deep and steadfast
connection to another person
which means through thick and thin
you remain connected it also
means in love there is no substitute. When you are in love with
your soulmate there is a profound spiritual connection. Profound
looks like where you are not close in
physical proximity your spirit
feels theirs. Often the heart aches for your soul mate and there
is actual pain because of the longing to be in close proximity.
You find that you will go to extreme lengths to close the physical
gap of space. This drawing is of the soul mates coming together
there is a dynamic closeness it is difficult to perceive one's lines
from the others. The beauty of soulmates there is no significant
comprehensive description. The drawing speaks for itself.

When Souls Touch

When souls touch
They vibrate a resonance
that electrifies the
atmosphere that they
are present in.

It does not matter
the length of time or the
duration of the encounter,
there is a knowledge
of the other
and an excitement
In the air.

The resonance of the
Soul's vibrations
want to, desires to touch
and be touched,
to touch and touch again.
It is the spiritual and physical
but it is the spiritual that
will last forever.

When Souls touch
You just can't get
enough of one another,
Always looking for

opportunities, to touch
and touch again.

It is not, yet is physical
the physical touch ads
another dimension to the
Soul's vibrations,
The vibrations resonate and
begin to dance and sing out of joy
because the souls
have found one another.

One wishes that it could
be just any soul,
It is not happen chance
the souls are drawn
Together from a magnetic
pull which vibrates.
No matter if it seems happen chance.

The soul's vibrations
Go from one to another
Looking for that which it is
Which attracts the soul?
Where its vibration resonates
When souls touch
The spiritual melds with Physical
and an awesome
Bond is formed.

The resonance of the
Soul's vibrations
Which touch the heart?
And lift the spirit
Transcends space and time
The soul does hunger and
Thirst for its completeness.

Children are our most treasured gift from God. It takes love, nurturing and chastising in order to raise them into successful adults. The job of loving and raising a child is one of the most challenging jobs we are blessed with.
The proverb says, "It takes a
village to raise a child". I took advantage
of all the help offered to
me while raising my children. I realized
that the elders along with
my mother, aunts and uncles had more experience and therefore, could offer sound and valuable advice.
I feel that somewhere along the path of raising children
that become social deviants something went extremely wrong.
Of course, there are individuals born with psychological issues, however, perhaps if identified early
society would not have as many
casualties as we have had in the recent past.

#1 Bald Eagle

I took this picture when I lived on the channel I realize that you probably will not get it but I had to try it reminds me. Of a certain tattoo. I hope you get this be blessed.

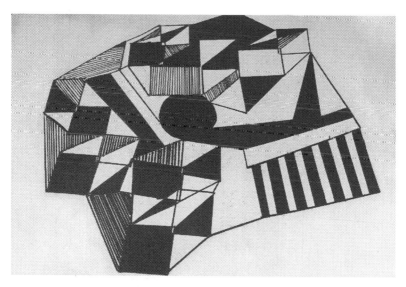

#2 Remembering my First Art class

Remembering my Freshman Art class where I could not even draw an apple on the white board in class, which brought me to tears because I was mortified because this should have been something very easy. Nevertheless, it was not I could not get a handle on drawing up on the white board instead of down on a desk. To make matters worse, I was a cheerleader and had on my uniform people already perceive that cheerleaders are empty-headed. As I returned to my seat through a haze of tears an upper classman/student teacher who I feel now was S.S. (at the time I could not even see his face through the blur of tears) called me aside and stated that he wanted to show me a simple trick. I could barely see where I was going because of the tears. He said it would only take a couple of minutes. I walked over to where he sat and watched him show me how to draw boxes that were three-dimensional. I practiced and low and be hold I could do it after five minutes. I might not be able to draw an apple but I could draw three-dimensional boxes. I had no idea exactly what to create using these boxes at that time. Today I have created lovely drawings and paintings with these boxes.

#3 Introduction to Art

I was taught how to draw this box after a very humiliating experience. I say this to state that perhaps not all students have the same artistic abilities but there is something that they can do which will show their genius. Today my painting and drawing skills have developed tremendously. I think my brain has rewired itself due to the diagnosis of M.S. and now I am good. Not all students will have the same abilities therefore, it be hooves teachers to find out where they excel. I must admit that B was a great teacher he also showed me how to draw something I could draw well, annamae horses. My thanks to S.S. and B for their kindness and patience.

#4 It Took Mr. B So Long

I feel that one of the reasons it took Mr. B so long to get back to me regarding his drawing was because I was struggling in his art class. When I was admitted to his class I suggested to him not to feel bad if he found it necessary to fail me because I recognized that I was really bad at drawing and painting. During his class my technique was poor however, I was very creative. I think he would be thoroughly floored to see a drawing and painting with superior technique. I must admit that it is the best painting that I have ever painted. I gaze at it often because I am so amazed that it is good.

#5 I Wish that B Was...

I wish that B was available to see this drawing of him I have developed tremendously since I was in his art class. This drawing is a good rendition of the painting. The painting in my estimation is good I am sure it will astound him when he can truly see it. I am sure he will be moved by my ability to capture his likeness in the painting. I have really progressed since taking his class. I was having challenges in painting my progress exemplified by this painting is an example of what teachers want to see happen with their student's. I am now engaged to marry him and I feel that the reason the painting turned out so well is because I am in love with him. I am amazed myself I never envisioned that I would have the ability to draw and paint.

#6 My Next Major Synchronicity

My next major synchronicity that truly shows me how God works was when I met Lady E. She was a well dressed lady over middle age who I encountered on my train ride back from Sacramento visiting my brother and his family. After boarding the train as I walked down the isle of the coach on the upper level a woman who was already seated whose name I came to know as lady E, looked at me and smiled. I smiled back, the coach was nearly empty because I was one of the first to board. Lady E, caught my eye smiling asked me if I would like to be her seat mate? I was surprised because not only was Lady E causation but because no one had ever asked me if I would like to be their seat mate. I thought this was novel and very polite. I remember thinking that I would have to ask a passenger the next time I boarded a train if they would like to be my seat mate. But of course I never remembered to ask.

As I took my seat next to Lady E, we began a great very cordial conversation about our lives. We found out that we both had a lot in common. One of the most memorable examples of what we shared is that her husband had recently passed he had been an accountant. Interestingly my uncle had just passed he also worked with numbers. He was an account rep for a firm. As we moved out of the train station our conversation continued to flow.

Lady E, shared information about her grandson who was attending college back East working on a degree in Art. I found this fascinating because I had recently told my aunt who is an artist that I was interested in taking an Art class. I shared with Lady E, when I was in High School as a Freshman I was terrible in Art. I couldn't even draw an apple. My aunt said I had a good eye and perhaps I had developed artistic ability since high school because I was able to capture aesthetically pleasing images through photography.

Lady E, continued the discussion about her grandson. She was hoping he would quickly complete his degree and return home as soon as possible she confided that he had a child to take care of.

Our conversation never lagged and before we knew it she was getting off the train. Before she left she told me that her grandson and I would get along well because we had common interests like art and film. I smiled and responded that I was sure I would get along fine with her grandson. I absolutely thought I would never meet her grandson in a million years. Before she left she told me her grandson's name. I was astounded so I repeated it twice, she smiled and said yes. So of course I would never forget his name because it was very prominent that is why I needed to repeat it for clarification.:).

I really liked Lady E, and felt that was a wonderful experience on the train. Most often when I ride the train I really don't remember the people I have spoken with not so with Lady E, we became friends during that short train ride to our destinations.

After Lady E, for the next three years I really did not encounter anyone like Lady E. Many of my seat companions were nice but we did not become friends as I did with Lady E. Therefore, 3 years after meeting Lady E, I had an incredulous meeting which was a major synchronicity. Most often I sit in the trains upper coach . For some reason which I don't remember at this time, I decided to sit on the lower level. There were a lot of people on this train several students from the local university and local community colleges.

I struck up a brief conversation with one of the male passengers to be friendly. (Of course he was definitely cute.) I asked him where he was headed he stated an area close to my destination. I responded that I lived in that area and attended Jr. High, High school and college in that area.

I noticed he had a tattoo on his chest. I asked him what it was, he opened his shirt and showed me the most amazingly beautiful tattoo of an eagle I had ever seen. I continue to remember it today. The art and colors were exquisite, the colors were bold and vivid. My breath caught in my throat at viewing such a beautiful creation. All I could do was stare and say I'm afraid of tattoos because there is pain involved. What I did not say was thank you for sharing with me because I was virtually a stranger however, because he shared it made me feel close to him. I was very impressed at the Eagle tattoo on his chest it was larger than life.

I collected my thoughts and asked him what he did for a living. He stated that he taught Art at the Community College a couple of cities from our location. My mind began to race, I thought can this man possibly be Lady E's grandson who was a student at a university back East getting his degree in Art? What are the chances that after 3 years of catching the train that I would catch the same train as Lady E's grandson, sit in the same coach on the same level at the same time on the same day? What are the chances one in a million.

As I was leaving the train I asked what his name was he told me the same name as Lady E's grandson and preceded to give me his business card. I told him that I was going to take his art class because I had been thinking about taking an Art class again. He smiled and was cordial never really believing that I would drive from where I lived just to take his Art class. Well he was wrong. I just had to find out if this man was Lady E's grandson.

Of course I got all kinds of flack from my family. I felt that I was an adult and could make my own life choices. So what if I wanted to take a class that was way out of the way it was my choice. What my family did not understand was that I had to find out if he was Lady E's grandson. My family wanted me to take an Art class closer to home. I told my family that this was an adventure, I had to come clean and tell my mom about the professor. I never would have believed that I would encounter so much resistance. I emailed the professor and informed him that I was signing up for his class, he responded that was welcome to take his class.

Therefore, this is just what I did, at the same time I was working on a Master's Degree.

Parking was atrocious at his Community College therefore, I was late getting to class. When I entered the class he smiled and suggested that I sit while he took attendance. I sat beside another student who was also waiting to see if he would allow her to enter the class. After some moments of tensely waiting he told us both that we would be admitted to the class.

Now my worry was how am I going to find out if Lady E, is his grandmother? I looked at the directory of teachers locations I located his address and wrote him a letter about my encounter with Lady E, I asked him if Lady E could possibly be his grandmother one week after I sent the letter.

#7 The First Man I Met on the Train
1/23/19

The first man I met while ridding the train was MM. He was an extremely handsome man about 28 or 30. I don't remember how we began our conversation however, I do remember what he was wearing. He wore a sky blue shirt and tan dockers, I seem to remember his shoes were dark brown loafers.

Perhaps I began the conversation with him because his hair was the same color red as my younger sister. Red heads run on my father's side of the family my cousin had a red haired son who gave birth to a red haired daughter. He as a young man was called red by his friends.

Getting back to M M, I was somewhat taken aback by the sheer beauty of his physical appearance, to be more explicit he was 6'3 at least, broad shoulders with an appropriate size waist. He was Caucasian his skin tone was very appealing sort of a golden hue. He is one of the most attractive men I have ever met. I remember thinking wow, he was well educated and a business man by the look of his briefcase.

During the course of our conversation we exchanged pleasantries I found that he was into creating a better world through cleaning up the environment. He impressed me because during the course of our conversation. I learned he had graduated from law school, but preferred environmental science. I am taking the slow route to make a major point, he waited for me when he could have just walked away I will explain this statement shortly.

#8 Trees are Our Life Blood

Trees are our life blood, the roots are great examples of strength and consistency.

#9 This painting resembles a close friend

This drawing is a work in process.

This is a drawing that resembles a friend. He is a very important friend because he protects me and makes sure all is well with me. I worked for his mother and she was as very kind to me while I worked for the Peace Corps. Working for his mother was one of the greatest opportunities I have been blessed to obtain. She was kind and also took an interest in my well-being while I was in Washington D.C. Before, I left the Peace Corps I was offered the position running the San Diego branch I regretfully had to turn it down. I was so honored and humbled that I had been offered such a prestigious position.

#10 Peace Corps Director Loret Ruppe Miller

Peace Corps Director Loret Ruppe Miller during my tenure with the Peace Corps. Photo of her and I signed by Mrs. Miller.

#11 Gleaners

Gleaners I painted. Millets' original painting is housed in the Louvre in Paris.

#12 Cross Design
2/14/19

Cross Design I created by observing several different motifs.

#13 Painted Boxes
2/13/19

Painted boxes, in sky blue, avocado green, black and white. These boxes are 3 dimensional.

#14 Little French Girl

Sketch and painting of a little French girl in a blue coat drawn and painted by me similar to Renoir.

#15 La Promenade

La Promenade based on a master painter's painting I painted this painting.

#16 Celtic icons & Poseidon

This drawing is based on Celtic icons & Poseidon.

#17 Joggers on the Beach
2/13/19

This is a fantastic photo because it shows movement the runners are in sync.

#18 Bird with Flower Petals for Feathers
2/14/19

I drew this bird in class, I felt combing flower pedals as feathers is unique.

#19 One of My First Paintings

This is one of my first paintings completed during my first year taking art in school.

#20 Family Photograph

Family photograph – my mother, aunt Glen and aunt Joe.

#21 Flight of Sea Gulls

#22 Puppy Cloud Formation

The formation is clear and very amazing. I always wonder if man had something to do with this formation.

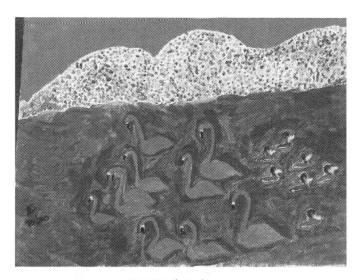

#23 Pink Pelicans

Pink Pelicans created during my first year of painting.

#24 Polka Dotted Bird Tail
2/15/19

When I first observed them I could not believe what I was seeing.

#25 Crane in Flight?
2/15/19

I am not certain this is a crane.

#26 My Mentor, My Teacher

My mentor, my teacher, my first large painting. I paint slowly therefore, I think this painting took 3 to 4 months to complete.

#27 Soulmates and Sketch
2/15/19

The sketch is of a couple who are wrapped as one.

#28 Three Dimensional Boxes
2/15/19

Painted boxes which are 3 dimensional boxes, yellow, burgundy & gray. This painting is based on the concept of boxes. They are not traditional boxes however, the placement of the boxes gives an illusion of three dimensions. The painting of the boxes further illustrates their three dimensionality.

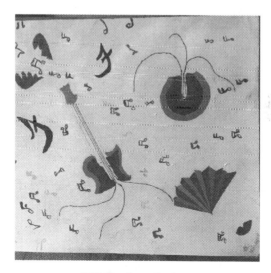

#29 Broken Strings
2/19/19

Musicians often break the strings to instruments; this can also be reflections of broken relationships.

#30 The Baby Edward, Prince of Wales
2/19/19

I fell in love with the photo of the painting of this baby so I had to capture him on canvas.

#31 Lincoln

2/19/19

#32 Charlotte Mecklenburg-Strelitz (Sophia Charlotte), wife of King George III
2/21/19

There are several reasons I drew this picture she is of African and European decent, she touched my heart because she opened a maternity hospital for women which exists today. Original portrait by Nathaniel Dance-Holland. She was also a botanist who worked on the expansion of Kew Gardens, she "provided funding to the General lying in Hospital in London which prevented its closure; it is named Queen Charlotte's and Chelsea Hospital."

1st edition

Contents

Preface to the Poems

The poems in this book are always about someone who has impacted my life in a positive way. The impact of the individual was and is heartfelt and deep, and the connection was made. This connection was powerful and therefore needed to be expressed in some form or manner, a soulful connection often makes for beautiful poetry.

When Souls Touch

When souls touch
They vibrate a resonance
That electrifies the
Atmosphere that they
Are present in.

It docs not matter
The length of time or the
Duration of the encounter,
There is a knowledge
Of the other
And an excitement
In the air.

The resonance of the
Soul's vibrations
Want to, desires to touch
And be touched,
To touch and touch again.
It is the spiritual and physical
But it is the spiritual that
Will last forever.

When Souls touch
You just can't get
Enough of one another,
Always looking for
Opportunities, to touch
And touch again.

It is not, yet is physical
The physical touch ads
Another dimension to the
Soul's vibrations,
The vibrations resonate and
Begin to dance and sing out
Of joy
Because the souls
Have found one another.

One wishes that it could
Be just any soul,
It is not happen chance
The souls are drawn
Together from a magnetic
Pull which vibrates
No matter if it seems happen chance

The soul's vibrations
Go from one to another
Looking for that which it is
Which attracts the soul?
Where its vibration resonates
When souls touch
The spiritual melds with
Physical and an awesome
Bond is formed.

The resonance of the
Soul's vibrations
Which touch the heart?
And lift the spirit

Transcends space and time
The soul does hunger and
Thirst for its completeness

By Naola Davis
May 15, 2010

Photograph by Naola Davis

What Is It?

What is it that
Makes my smile radiate
From ear to ear,
Is it a smile or
The crinkle of his eyes
When his gentle smile
Envelopes my entire countenance?

What is it about
The one who is but
Is not supposed to be
Try as I might I
Can't suppress the giddy
Feeling that encompasses
My heart,
Thou it should not
Be so,

What it is pure
Joy and pure delight
To have feelings
With no way of fulfilling
The possible ecstasy or odyssey
Just because it is.

What is it that
Happens, but what is it
That does not happen
When it should

Because there is something
That should not be there
But is, which stifles
The essence of what is supposed to be
But is not.

What is it that
Happens when the joy
No longer envelopes your
Entire being with a look or a smile.

What is it when
Your heart breaks in half
After longing for that
Which is no more?
Your heart,
Moans and groans
In its longing
For that which was?
But is no more.

What is it that
Drives me to recapture
The love that once
Was, but cannot be
Anymore.

Death has a way
Of ending the physical
Relationship, the spiritual
Relationship is never over
Until you cross over and
Connect, and join the one

Who once was?
And now joins you dancing
On the astral rainbow
Forever more.

June 24, 2010
By Naola Davis

Acknowledgements

Of course when you thank the people who have helped you on this journey invariably someone is left out, I have several people to thank for their input and help with strengthening me on this path, of course number one is God, 2nd my mother Ola Washington for assistance. 3rd my sister she planted seeds before she passed, my aunt Mary who first read my book from cover to cover, my aunt Joe who has made the struggle easier, and my children who I love with all of my heart; and Rob who gave me the courage to complete my book, for the past two years I have had a friend who has been instrumental in keeping me balanced even though he did not realize it, and Sean for introducing me to a career that I could incorporate my teaching skills and help others while making money at the same time. I know I am leaving someone out, but for all of those who I know and love, thank you for your kindness and support.

Thanks to Louis Washington for support and Julia Dixon my best friend. Special thanks to Weldon Washington and Shauna Robinson and Nathan Davis and his wife Blanca Quintero.

Prologue

My journey on the path to Spiritual Enlightenment began at a very young age; at the age of one and a half; I was violently thrust into the arena of good and bad, violent and non-violent in order to cope with the violence in my life, I connected with my "source." Outwardly, I was a "happy-go-lucky," child, while inwardly trying to rationalize, and trying to understand how a person, like my father, who walked the earth, could grow into a monster, because for the most part we all start out as good human beings. There are some cases where a soul is born with an evil predisposition, but for the most part, people start out good, the environment they are born into plays a large role in shaping the person they ultimately become. Sanaya Roman states,

> "The awakening of man is the journey into awareness of the higher energy realms. Many people had painful childhoods, not understanding how to deal with the rigidity or negativity you found around you."

I was fortunate to be born into a family with a visible dichotomy, my father was a violent rigid man who took his anger and frustration with life (his environment), out on my mother; my mother, Vivian on the other hand is a beautiful, kind and loving soul, through the help of God maintained her humanity, sanity, and dignity while suffering many indignities that my father brutalized her with, which in turn taught me how to deal with an abusive spouse, we learn from our parents through their success and failures. Through it all God was and is our strength and salvation which is what my mother was taught by her mother, Big

Momma, who was taught by her mother Isabel Higgins, who was taught by her mother Sally Higgins.

Having been born into a family of prayer warriors is obviously a blessing, but it was also a blessing to have been born not only to my mother but my father also. Because of the violence perpetrated on my mother by my father, my sister passed, therefore I was spoiled and given everything I desired, these events shaped me, into a somewhat spoiled extraverted person in my youth introverted, and contemplative during the later years; violence had indicated to me that there would be times in my life when I would have to fall down on my knees and pray. And though, it was not easy, I learned that with God on your side no one can defeat you.

Through life's many toils and snares, I have found that being taught how to pray was one of the most fundamental skills to have during a crisis when there is no one to turn to, no one to help ease your pain; although man can take away all of your earthly goods, no one can take your ability to reason; nor your joy, and happiness or your ability to pray and call on the lord during your hours of desperation. This doesn't mean you only pray when there is turmoil in your life but through joy and pain.

Prayer is visible in its movement just as the wind is visible while blowing leaves, trees and dust. You cannot see the wind, but you can feel the wind as it blows on your face, as you can feel the presence of God when he moves in your soul. As you can see the results of the wind as it blows, you can see the results of the father when he moves in your life; making a way out of no way, when there does not seem to be anywhere to turn, the father opens up a way that had been previously closed. That is the miraculous way the father works.

Therefore throughout the course of this book, I discuss the various episodes of my life that have made a major impact on my evolution, in so doing, created the person that I am today, continuously learning and growing in order to refine my soul so that when I die I can become one with the father. Moreover through the course of this book, I allude to my "spiritual amnesia" (Kim O'Neill) as a result of my experiences. Initially (believe it or not) I have a vague memory of promising never to forget what I was to do when I reached my earthly destination, though I never forgot, I became paralyzed by the fear of not getting it right, not doing what I was sent here to do. ONeill maintains,

> Spiritual amnesia causes people to agonize over their life's purpose, wallow in dysfunction, and remain ignorant about issues they need to resolve. Spiritual amnesia creates within us an anxiety-ridden gnawing fear of setting higher goals, taking greater risks, meeting new challenges, opening completely to a personal relationship.

During my paralysis, I simply just let bills go, the maintenance of contracts, relationships go un-nurtured, although I have always been aware of what needed to be completed, I did not have the energy nor motivation to complete those seemingly mundane tasks, also I did not realized that the brutalization of my mother, brutalized me in turn. There is something about the protective mechanism of disconnection, which allows you not to feel the full impact, or even remember events that are too painful. However today is a new day, and through counseling, reading self-help books and God, I have taken back control of my life. Though I am far from perfect, I continuously strive to be the best person I can be, many may not realize what I am striving to achieve because I do not verbalize it and I know the father realizes and completely understands what I am striving for in this life, I would hope through my actions, "which speak louder than words,". Proverbs NIV 4:20-23 & 26 states:

> "my son pay attention to what I say;
> Listen closely to my words.
> Do not let them out of your sight,
> Keep them within your heart;
> For they are life to those who find them
> And health to a man's whole body.
> Above all else guard your heart,
> For it is the well spring of life.
> 26 Make level paths for your feet."

And so this is the story of my journey on the Path to enlightenment in order to have a closer walk with God. I don't know much, and there is still much to know but this is how my search, my quest began, and this is where it has taken me.

During my search I have discovered synchronicities which take place in our everyday lives moreover many people know when they have encountered an event which makes them stand in awe, because you have encountered God's hand placing two events in your life that you know is not an accident, in conversation you mention someone's name and the telephone rings immediately and the person you mentioned is on the telephone. There are many times when I have witnessed the hand of God working miracles in my life and the lives of others.

For example when we left Germany, we moved to Washington State because Sergeant had been redeployed for another stint at a base in Washington, through a series of events, my mother became best friends with a woman named Kyra. After a series of discussions one day they were talking and discovered that they had relatives with the same names, Kyra told Vivian, that when her mother came to visit her from New Mexico, they would ask her what she knew about Kyra's great aunt who had the same name as Vivian's grandmother aka Mother Dear. They found out that their grandmother's were sisters.

Another example of synchronicity was when I taught, I joined a women's organization, the girls that were sponsored in this organization became debutantes, and the girls were taught how to become ladies, proper etiquette. One of the young ladies Jocelyn needed a ride home after an event, I volunteered to take her home because I had known her previously, and she had been a student in my United States, "History Class". I asked her the address to her home she told me a very familiar address, 1234 West Iris Street, I said how is that possible, I lived at that address when was in the 5ᵗʰ grade.

Also when I lived in Washington D.C. after graduating from college, I worked for the Peace Corps and I took a second job because living in Santa Barbara and attending the university, I had very few dress clothes, therefore I got a job at a dress shop in the George Town Park Mall; one day when I was waiting on one of my customers, who was very friendly, we began to talk.

She asked me where I was from, I told her Santa Barbara California, and we both thought we looked familiar, well as luck would have it, she was one of my mother's friends and she remembered me from her association with my mother. She had become an attorney for the United States Postal Service.

This was another major synchronicity that took place in my life. There have been so many synchronicities during my life and the lives of family members I don't have enough paper to mention them all.

However, another major synchronicity occurred during the 70's, the U.S. economy was floundering, there were long lines at the gas station, frustration was so ramped that it was visible in the air. It was like a huge dark cloud that was hanging over the U.S. especially California.

In the midst of the frustration there was also irony, and excitement, it was like an electric current moving through society. People were losing their jobs and homes, the people who kept their homes saw the value of their homes plummet, like an anchor pulling, dragging down the economy.

In this arena a very interesting event took place, I would describe this synchronicity as a (meet cute) however it does not completely fit the criteria. This leads me to the meeting of a man who has played a significant role in my life for many years. I know that God knows what is going to happen in my life before it ever occurs, some say providence, I say God.

The event which unfolded was truly amazing, reflecting back and remembering the event as it happened, I know God was in the midst. The set of circumstances that intertwined this chance meeting was nothing but God; the supreme force that connects all mankind to one another.

As I mentioned previously gasoline shortage, along with this supermarket strikes were taking place. During this time I was 19 and already the mother of a one ½ year old, living with my girlfriend from High School Julia, and already divorced from my daughter's father who resided in Oklahoma. I have always been independent and a take charge type of person, however event with these attributes I was not socially aplomb at times. When it came to living and taking care of my daughter that reigned supreme; therefore I was not as socially conscious as I am today. Therefore, since my daughter needed milk and diapers, not only did I cross the picket line I took one of the poor striker's jobs.

I was not receiving any child support from my daughter's father, I eventually had to take him to court and file for divorce and child support, to say the least, I needed the money. I have always believed in working, however today I would never replay my prior actions.

To set the stage more clearly, I had just quit working for a nursing home, I had the graveyard shift, and physically, I could not handle the hours. Therefore, to make a buck I crossed the picket line. I could not believe that after I applied that I was hired. Crossing the picket line was no easy task, there was a shove or two and name calling, but I made it inside of the location for my new job, which was very short lived.

After the two days that I worked for Alpha Beta, sacking grocery, which was a very demanding job, my hat is off to checkers I give them my respect, it is a labor intensive job. (It doesn't look like it but it is.) It was during this time, while I was sacking grocery that I noticed an African American young man trying to make eye contact; I pretended not to see him. He dressed casually, in a green army jacket, shorts and thongs.

Max as I came to know later moved through the line and I bagged his grocery. Even though I did not make eye contact he asked for my phone number. I said no when I wanted to say yes. It was not that he was bad looking, he was very handsome in a Eddie Murphy kind of way.

After he did not get my number I thought that would be the end of it. I don't even think I got his name, however I just chalked it up to meeting a guy who wanted my phone number. That was not the end of it however, after I returned home at about 9:00, the phone rang, and of course I answered it, (I did not ignore phone calls until later). The caller was a man looking for his cousin in Texas named Shelia. Because the caller was looking for his cousin in Texas named Shelia, I was intrigued on several levels. First, I was born in Texas. So instead of hanging up I questioned him.

He again said he was looking for his cousin named Shelia, I told him that I have a cousin in Texas named Shelia. I asked what part of Texas, he said either Dallas or Houston, I replied, my cousin lives in Dallas. This to me seemed very coincidental so we decided to meet that same evening. After we exchanged addresses I told my roommate that we were going to have a visitor, I told her that it was a man that had accidentally called looking for his cousin. Her and I cracked up, what a way to get a date. He said that he would be over in an hour, however this was not the case, one hour went into two, and after about two hours the doorbell rang. When I opened the door, to my surprise, it was the same guy that had been flirting at the grocery store. He was as surprised as I was, but I just wondered if he had somehow gotten my phone number from management in the store. So I smiled and invited him in and asked, "how did you get my number," he said "it was an accident, I did not know who you were when I dialed the number, you were supposed to be my cousin."

Chapter 1

"Who will die?"

I was born on a cold day in November; I was named after my mother, Vivian and my father, Sergeant, which was combined to create Vanda. My mother said when she saw me; she thought she should have named me Sergeant Jr. because I looked so much like my father. Every time she made this comment, I would ignore her, (I couldn't detach from this) it hurt my feelings so badly to be that closely associated with my father in terms of my looks. I knew that I looked like him, I just did not want to be reminded that I looked like the man that I found it difficult to love, because of his violent nature.

My mother was very religious and spiritual, my father was a military man, however, he was raised in church as a young child, he believed in God though you could hardly tell, he rarely if ever attended church. My father ensured that he left his mark on me by being an alcoholic, violent, disrespectful man towards almost all women especially me and my mother. My mother's education and religious background, helped prepare me for what I was to become, an educated, spiritual, intuitive woman, perhaps also somewhat psychic, and a conduit for healing.

The first few years of my life were rife with violence and various types of disease and illness. Physically, I looked like my father, my mother said that when she first saw me she could see very little of herself in me which was compounded by well meaning people, who good naturedly asked if my father was Japanese or Chinese. My father looked Chinese in his features especially his eyes. As I grew older, which I have found, was a major feat because it appeared, as a child I might succumb to one of my childhood illnesses.

I was less than one when I had my first bout with double pneumonia, it was during this period that my mother had given birth to my sister, Yvonneka Suzette, she was born on another cold day in November, unfortunately my sister, who I would have shared my birth month with, was born without a rectum. Therefore when I was hospitalized with double pneumonia, my new born sister was also hospitalized in hopes that a rectum could be created for her. Generally when there are birth defects, spouses have a tendency to blame one another, as was the case with baby Yvonneka's birth defect.

Sergeant was a product of the military, he knew one course of action well, and that was how to be a solider, which does not necessarily make a good spouse or father. Because of this, my father would goad my mother during the early stages of their marriage and at times place her in uncomfortable situations in order to watch her squirm, such as were done to him during his stint in the military. Oklahoma can be a very hostile land, especially if you go exploring some of the snake and eel infested swamps which is what my father did, dragging my pregnant mother along with him. Reportedly, she had never been so scared in her entire life, apparently just to watch the snakes and eels as they glided across the swamp was too tame, he did what most "real men" would have done, rowed across the swamp, inviting the snakes and eels to nip at the boat. If he were not with his wife, and if he were instead just hanging out with some of his army buddies, this would have been dangerous but excusable exercise in manhood prowess, however, totake a pregnant woman across a swamp infested with snakes and eels is indicative of the major character flaws he possessed which were dramatized throughout his life.

Of course, my mother blamed the swamp escapade on my

sister's deformity, my father did not say much regarding the causes of Yvonneka's malformed rectum, he took her death hard because he was ready to have the second baby, the first one, he had not been ready to father, he was too busy "running the streets and chasing women."

Prior to Yvonneka's death, I had been admitted to the hospital, we were still living in Oklahoma and I was reportedly playing as though nothing was wrong, when I leaned against the refrigerator and slowly slid down the front. My mother of course, ran over to me saying, "What's the matter Vanda baby; is something wrong." She felt my head and I was burning up with a high fever.

Most mothers have to be strong women, my mother had to be stronger than most during this time in her life, it was only with the grace of God that she was able to survive what she had to encounter. She had two babies in the hospital at the same time, my new born sister and me, I was diagnosed with double pneumonia and an oxygen tent was placed around my bed, it looked like my bed was wrapped in a cellophane tent.

Yvonneka was flown to San Antonio for an experimental new surgery, in the hopes that she would be able to survive at such a young age, two months old, as surgeons tried to create a rectum for her. While the surgery was being performed on Yvonneka, I had a prolonged stay in the hospital to recuperate from double pneumonia; it is termed double because both lungs are infected. One day during this time period, my mother received a phone call from the hospital, "Vivian we regret to inform you but your baby is dead." My mother's heart dropped, and she immediately thought "dear God I hope it's not the baby that I have gotten to know." She asked when she could recover some what, "which baby?" "Your baby; which was flown to San Antonio military hospital, for orthopedic surgery, Yvonneka. (I named my daughter Yvonneka Suzette, after my sister). My mother was heart broken over the loss of Yvonneka, she was upset with God because he had let her baby die, however, she was pleased in another sense that it was not the baby that she had spent the past year with.

If there was ever a time in my mother's life when she felt that God had forsaken her, it was during this period of time; there were many events that would take place in her life that had tried her faith and trust in the Father; the major event was the death of baby, Yvonneka. The Dr. recommended that she have another baby right away and not a long time, a baby would help her heal more rapidly and not allow her to prolong her grieving for the loss of her child.

Chapter 2

The Replacement Baby

My mother did as the Dr. had suggested and quickly got pregnant with her third child, Gigi. For as long as I can remember Gigi had an attitude, she wouldn't smile for pictures, she would dump her breakfast (oatmeal) over her head, she was just not a happy camper. My father loved Gigi; she was the replacement baby, for the baby they had lost.

My father had moved us from Oklahoma to Stuttgart Germany, my mother and I sailed to Germany on an Ocean Liner, while on board the boat my mother was taught how to Cha-cha by some of the "Fresh" Stuarts. I, did poorly on the Ocean Liner, I threw up constantly. I loved the feel of the cool sea breeze on my face, therefore I would pull a stool close to the porthole and stick my head out of the little round hole, on one occasion my mother happened to return to our room as I tittered off balance and almost fell into the ocean. I was severely reprimanded for scaring my mother; the rest of the journey was uneventful.

Chapter 3

Oma and Opa

My father met us when we arrived, I would not speak to him or give him a hug, he had brought me a gift that I did not like but he brought my mother a white gold diamond ring. I told him, "I want a ring." And he basically dismissed me and the entire incident and went on to respond to my mother; therefore, I would not kiss or hug him on our arrival. During our stay in Germany we lived with a German family, Oma and Opa, my mother and I learned German. While we lived with Oma and Opa we were a part of their family even though we were just U.S. government renters.

One day I went into the kitchen while Oma was putting freshly baked bread and butter on the table. I loved Oma's bread and butter, even though our family had a lot of food; we had bacon and eggs, bread and butter also, I wanted Oma's bread and butter. Oma put her bread and butter on the table. Oma wanted me to stop, she said, Du, Du Vanda, Du kheigt aber howie. (Oma was stating that if I did not stop she was going to give me a spanking.) I responded, pee, pee Oma. Oma went into my mother's bedroom and asked her, "Vivian vas ist das, pee, pee?" She explained what she had said to me. My mother explained "One muss enrolle machten wassen kompt; ween dass wasser kompt das ist pee pee." (My mother explained the difference between pee and BM.) Once Oma understood she laughed until tears rolled down her face. Oma was a kind, silver gray haired 70 year old woman. Oma and her husband had migrated from (Czechoslovakia.) Their family owned a two story home in which they rented out space to the United States government, Oma and Opa's adult daughter Marianna and her daughter Isolde, also stayed in rooms in the two story home. It made for a great cultural exchange between the nations represented.

Chapter 4

The violence raged with the Diary of Ann Frank

My father became more abusive given the freedom of a foreign land, I remember standing behind my mother one morning after my father had been abusive, and she was in the bathroom looking in the mirror trying to fix her face. Her eyes were swollen and her lip had been busted, "Mom, what are you doing?" "Trying to make my face look better." "Why? Your face always looks nice, what happened to your face?" "Your daddy beat me up?" "Why?" "He was drinking and that is what he does at times when he gets drunk." I went out of the house singing a song that I didn't know the significance of, "My daddy beat my mommy up?" "My daddy beat my mommy up! This was the beginning of my disassociating from painful incidents, turning it around making the event appear as though something good had taken place instead of something awful, because as a two year old child, I could not deal with how painful and awful the reality of the situation was. I had to make it something light and fun so that I wouldn't feel the pain that was very close to my heart.

This really nasty event took place when my mother and her girlfriend went to see the Diary of Anne Frank; the movie's showing time was two hours which was much longer than other movies. When my mother arrived home my father was furious, she tried to explain that she had spent the entire 2 hours at the movies, but he would not listen. For some reason, he felt that she was doing what he was doing which was having other people, even though she was 9 months pregnant.

He was so furious at the thought that she could have been with another man that he could not contain his anger, my mother pleaded with him, she begged him not to hit her, but to no avail. He shouted, "I'll teach you to cheat on me, you bitch, after all I do to take care of you and Vanda." He backed her up, she tripped and fell on her bottom, and then he began to hit her in her face. He wanted her, (apparently) not to look so attractive to other men. She continued to plead, "Sergeant, no, don't, I swear I was at the movies the whole time." "I don't believe you; you were probably hanging out with some "Nigga" you picked up." "Please sergeant, no don't, what about the baby?" "I don't care about the baby; she needs to see you get your butt beat so she will know how to behave when she gets older." With that, he forced her on her back and straddled her pregnant belly and beat her in the face, as I stood in the corner of the room watching, tears silently flowed down my face because I didn't know what to do, I said "Daddy stop, stop Daddy, don't beat my mommy up." He continued to pound her in the face; I could not stand watching him beat my mother. I ran from the corner of the room and jumped on his back and told him to stop. I beat his back with my tiny fist, as he continued to beat up my mom. "Stop daddy I cried, don't beat my mommy up." And I continued to sock him in the back with my 2year old fist until finally, either I hit him hard enough or he heard me sobbing for him to stop, that he stopped. He placed me on the floor and told me he had to teach my mother a lesson and not to be like her so my future husband wouldn't be forced to give me a whipping. My memories of Germany are somewhat incomplete memories such as these have been repressed.

Chapter 5

Pneumonia

My mother loved Germany and the German people loved her, I continued to become deathly ill and experienced another bout of double pneumonia and again was placed in an Oxygen tent. My father was out in the field working on maneuvers when my temperature shot up past 105, my mother had no transportation and had to go door to door and ask for a ride to take her with her baby to the hospital. Finally my mother was able to ask one of the men in my father's battalion for a ride, he was a Southerner, he said "no I can't give you and your baby a ride to the hospital, I ain't got no gas." His wife came to the door and asked what my mom wanted, "My baby is sick, I have to get her to the hospital." The German woman looked at her husband and said, "Honey, we must take the baby to the hospital. We have to get the baby to the hospital." God was in the plan, had it not been for the German woman, my mother wouldn't have had a ride to the hospital. The diagnosis was touch and go after my mother arrived with me at the hospital I recovered after several weeks. These were the traumatic first few years of my life which have shaped the path I walk.

Chapter 6

Carbon Copy

My first husband was a direct result of violence and the disparaging remarks my father had made toward my mother, my choice of a husband was not one my mother could stomach because he was almost a carbon copy of my father. He was in the navy when I met him, he was born and raised in Oklahoma, and as his mother Thelma would say, "He had a bad understanding." which says so much about him. Little Prince was the first man that I had ever made love with, I met him at 17 and I was a virgin. I was so sheltered that I had never even seen an adult male penis; when I did see it, I was shocked that it was supposed to go inside of me. I was so sheltered that when I was sixteen, I finally got up the nerve to ask my mother a question that I had been dying to ask but I was too embarrassed. Although, I had seen sex education movies, I could never see or understand exactly where the male penis was to go. One day when my mother and sister were in the kitchen I asked my mother, "When men and women make love, where exactly does the penis go? Does it go in the pee, pee hole, or the booty hole? I had no idea, not a clue where it was supposed to go.

My mother looked at me incredulously, "You've got to be kidding?" "You mean to tell me that you don't know what hole a man's penis goes in? I looked at my mom and said, "I honestly don't have a clue." Then she says to Gigi my 14 year old sister, "Tell your sister the hole that the penis goes in." My sister tried to explain but couldn't explain it clearly enough. My mother, now exasperated stated, "Next time you go to the bathroom put your finger down there and feel around, there's another hole down there." I said, Oh, embarrassed. So when I met my ex husband at 17, and I saw his penis, I was shocked.

I was shocked because I thought the male's anatomy would look very similar to a babies, it didn't. As the virgin I was, I had no idea how he expected to get his penis in my vagina so I asked, "How do you think you will be able to get your penis in me?" He explained that I would stretch to meet his size, I said oh, but I was very leery. I married after one year and one baby at 18. He was violent, he was from the old school and he believed in spanking children. Once he had told our daughter to get up on the sofa, she was two years old, she was trying to get up on the sofa, but her little legs would not get her up there. He took off his belt and began to spank her. I said, "You see that she is trying to get up there, why would you spank her if she is doing what you asked?" "Don't interfere when I'm disciplining my daughter." I stood in front of my child, I told him "If you want to pick on someone, pick on someone your own size."

Well, to say the least I didn't just sit there and take it, I fought back, but he was a man, a small man but a man none the less. There is no way that I would ever let any man or woman abuse my child or anyone else's child. I dealt with him for two years, too long. During this time, I chose a man to date based on his looks not his character; he looked like the singer Prince. He had many character flaws; cheated on me by dating my girlfriend, I was miserable for the two years I lived in Oklahoma.

The last time I left, he almost busted a head gasket, as I was taking a bath before flying out of Oklahoma for the 20th time in two years, I reflected back on the conversation we had a few minutes before I got into the tub. As I was packing my suitcase to leave he said, "If you leave I'm sending you home in a box." Any body else would have gotten this, but I didn't. I didn't get it because how could the man that you married go from being in love, to threatening to put you in a box. As I sat in the tub washing my body preparing to return home, he entered into the bathroom. He was so angry, that I could see steam coming from his ears. I made the mistake of laughing; he said "so you think that's funny?" He grabbed my throat, and pushed my head under the water. My arms flailed violently in the air, because I was running out of Oxygen. My mind was racing, I thought to myself, he is actually going to kill me. When I was almost out of Oxygen, I thought "Oh God, here I come." The second I had that thought he let me up and laughed, "I bet you thought I was going to kill you?" And he actually laughed. At that moment, I told God, "If you let me leave, I promise I will never go back." Because I had previously left him and returned so many times, my family joked that I should own stock in American Airlines. God blessed me to leave and I never returned.

Chapter 7

Walking on God's
Straight and Narrow Path

I have often wondered if I was walking on God's straight and narrow path. There are times when I realize that I am in sync with the creator and more often then not; I realize I am walking on my own path. The question is where is my path leading and do I want to continue down my own path by myself?

I now know where the lord's path leads; it leads to fulfillment in this life and the next as stated in Psalms 23:3-5.

"Psalms 23:3-5

3. He leads me in the paths of righteousness
For His name's sake.
4. Yea, though I walk through the valley of the
shadow of death,
I will fear no evil,
For you are with me;
Your rod and staff, they comfort me.
5. You prepare a table before me in the
presence of my enemies;
You anoint my head with oil;
My cup runs over.
Surely goodness and mercy shall follow me
All the days of my life;
And I will dwell in the house of the LORD Forever.

And isn't that what we all want, fulfillment? Fulfillment means joy, peace and happiness through the most difficult of times and difficult times influence our spiritual growth, better known as Growing Pains. This is the period of time when your soul is reshaped and refined so that eventually we will be worthy of becoming one with the creator. Psalms 23:5 David maintains that his "cup runs over" meaning that he is so blessed by following the path of righteousness that he has enough worldly goods to satisfy more than himself. God says that he will protect and bless you all the days of your life if you walk the righteous path.

Righteousness will bring you closer to God and therefore at the end of your life, generally teenagers do not contemplate the end of their lives unless they are terminally ill or severely depressed. However as a young adult I thought about what takes place in this life and the next, and therefore I realized the importance of my actions along with having a just heart and a kind spirit. At the age of sixteen, which is supposed to be the best year of your life, because you are in the transition period between childhood and adult? No more wishing you were sixteen because now you are sixteen, at sixteen you can begin to wish you were eighteen, then twenty-one and after twenty-one we want to stop the sands of time, mid-stream because we have finally reached the legal age of an adult in the United States. At the age of sixteen our mortality is the last thing on our minds, we feel that we will not die for eons, that we will live fore ever.

Death is a most interesting occurrence, we all know that we must die and it is something that many of us fear, although a few people perceive correctly that when the body passes away, the soul crosses over to another dimension or level of existence. Most often for those who fear death it is because of the unknown, people have died and come back to tell us what they've, experienced, although near death experiences are thought to be fascinating, many do not want to move on to an unknown level of existence, moreover, they would like to hang on to material items and surroundings of this dimension. Whenever we hang on to material items of this dimension, people are included in material items, the soul is weighted down and transition to the next level of existence is difficult. When we get too wrapped up in materialism, our spirit will not want to let go of the material items of this world, therefore it will hinder our ascension. For example, if you love your home, there is the possibility that when you pass, you may not want to move on to the next level because you don't want to leave your home; the same is true of becoming too attached to people. Even with all the information there is today regarding what happens when you pass, many still fear death because of the unknown. However, King David states in Psalms 23:4 "Yea though I walk through the valley of the shadow of death, I will fear no evil, for you are with me." Therefore if you have followed the path of God during your life, you should not fear death because God is with you. Moreover, when you pass God is there to comfort, support and carry you through, you do not pass alone, and often a friend or relative is with you who passed previously. Elizabeth Clare Prophet writes about heaven in her book, *Kabbalah*,

> "Through his inner walk with God, Ezekiel made himself ready, and the quality of his readiness was acceptable in the sight of the Lord." "Imagine yourself as Ezekiel, a priest and captive in Babylon, settled with his fellow Judahites by the river Chebar. One day you look up And to your amazement the heavens are opened to you. The Lord allows you to see the seven planes of heaven And even himself. The Lord speaks directly and expressly To you, and he places his hand upon you."

Elizabeth Clare Prophet goes on to state,

> "This interchange happened to a son of man who walked the earth like you and me. What set him apart was the rightness of his heart, the integrity of his soul and the brilliance of his spirit."

Chapter 8

Many Deaths the summer of my 16th year

During the summer of my sixteenth year, I had cause to ponder and explore the reality of death. I had three very close friends die; cease to exist on this physical plane. And at sixteen I could not believe it; I could not believe my friends would never come back. After I went to the funeral of my first girlfriend who died, the second funeral, I neglected to attend which was that of her best friend, who was also a close friend of mine.

My first friend to die that summer was my boyfriend, he was a basketball player at my High School, and I was a cheerleader. I had left town and my best friend called me to let me know what had happened to Robby. He died riding a motorcycle that he had gotten for his birthday. I was out of town and I did not know of his death in time to attend to his funeral. Schaunna called me, she was my best friend during High School, she was (salt and I was pepper,) and relayed the news of Robby's death. Looking back, I can remember sadness but not profound, debilitating pain that often accompanies death. I think that I was in shock; I thought how could I return to school in the fall and not see him there, standing with his basketball buddies in the quad. My second friend to die the summer of my 16 year was Danna, A.K.A. Marietta.

My girlfriend Marietta, I could not believe that she had also died, especially the manner in which she died. She was fifteen and had gotten pregnant; her father was a military man like my father. Marietta and I were talking when we were in the 6th grade, I asked, "where were you born? Were you born here in Oxnard?" "No I was born in Texas." "So was I, I was born in a small town that no one has ever heard of." "So was I. What is the name of the small town you were born in?" "I don't want to say because no one has ever heard of the town." "I bet my town is smaller than yours" "Come on tell me the name of your town, no, I'll be embarrassed." "O.K. let's both say the name of our towns at the same time." We were surrounded by three of our other girlfriends. So they said that they would listen to hear the name of each of our towns since we were going to say it at the same time. One of our friends said "I'm going to count and on three you will both say the name of the town you were born in. The friend who volunteered to count was Sue Turner. O.K., ONE, TWO, THREE, "At first I could not hear what Marietta had said, but our friend who was listening said that she said, "Mineral Wells Texas." I said, "What? This has got to be a mistake, Marietta, what did you say?" "What did you say?, someone said you said "Mineral Wells Texas." "I did, Marietta, you were born in Mineral Wells Texas too?" "I can't believe that we were both born in the same small town in Texas. What are the chances that two girls who are one year apart in age would be born in the same small town in Texas and then meet each other when they are in the 6th grade because they both now live in another small town, but this time in Oxnard California?"

We laughed and ran to each other and gave one another a big hug. We felt in that instance that God's hand had somehow touched our lives and coordinated our destinies. We were always being told how much we looked alike; I found out later that there was a rumor that my father had gotten another soldier's wife pregnant. Now Marietta was pregnant, she was supposed to have her baby on the military base. It had been rumored that the military did not have well trained physicians; and something went dreadfully wrong while Marietta was in labor. The saddle block, (that is what epidurals were called at that time), which was to deaden from the waist down, was administered into the wrong vertebrae and deadened from the waist up, instantly killing her brain and her baby in her birth canal.

When I went to her funeral, I was told that the baby had a small coffin, which was underneath her pillow in her coffin. The strange thing about this funeral was that when I looked at Marietta, I noticed that the person (spirit) that I knew to be Marietta's was not there. I saw her body, but Marietta was not there, her body was bloated, she was not there. I mean, she was not in her body, it has been stated that the spirit stays around the body for at least three days before moving on, that may be so, but what made Marietta, Marietta, her spirit, soul and the animation which invigorated the body was not there. It was the shell that housed her spirit. It was at this time when I realized that you are so much more than your body. Often men and women get caught up in strengthening their bodies which is fine, but at the same time we need to be cognizant of the fact that we need to strengthen our spirit and soul. Marietta had a beautiful soul, nice, kind and gentle but at the same time strong; she was also vibrant and radiant along with having a great personality.

Many of her friends were at her funeral, including her best friend Tammie. Marietta, Tammie and I, were close friends in elementary school, we use to say that we were cousins when-ever people would ask if we were related. We had sleepovers at each other's houses, this was fun of course, we would have pillow fights and gossip about the other girls at our school, and of course we would discuss who we thought was the cutest boy at our school.

At the time of Marietta's funeral, I thought Tammie was fine, but I found out later from my aunt, who was a pediatric nurse (Janice) that Tammie was dying of Leukemia. I was surprised and shocked because she never said anything to me about being ill, nor did she ever complain. Tammie had always been thin, I had no idea that the reason that she was thin was because, after her treatments for Leukemia, she could not hold down her food. She never complained to me that there were any problems taking place in her life. My aunt Janice stated that Tammie's treatments were painful and the medication contributed to her inability to hold down her food. I have often felt that the cure is sometimes more difficult to handle than the illness itself.

We have all seen those commercials that state that they help to provide relief for some illness, the caveat in the commercial is if you take this drug you may experience some projectile vomiting, a rash, along with a migraine headache. Now tell me, which is worse the disease or the cure that can help with the disease, which is generally not 100% guaranteed.

One month later, Tammie died. I could not bring myself to go to the funeral. I knew that she would not be there, in the body. It was after this summer that I started to read everything I could about death and dying. It somehow gave me comfort to know that many people believe that this isn't the end to existence. Having had three people that I was close to die within a matter of three months, made me question where my friends went.

The questions I asked myself and God was, "where were my friends, where did their spirits go, or did they just cease existing, and would I ever see them again?" I have never read a book that stated that we just ceased to exist, perhaps that's because I chose not to read books that did not provide hope for the continuation of existence or the authors of those books were unable to find a publisher who would publish their work.

Chapter 9

Why Am I Here

Through my exploration, I did find some answers for my questions, not right away though; I had to have another death touch my heart, spirit and my soul before I found the answers to my questions. I feel that one of the most profound things in life is to have your soul touched significantly to the extent that it creates questions which you must find the answers to in order to be at peace within yourself. I am working on myself as many are who dream of reaching this level of evolution.

For example; *why am I here? "Am I here on earth just to explore the earthly plane? Am I here just to get through life, and if so what does it mean to my soul to get through life? Should I take others along with me as I traverse dense plane, or should we evolve to a place where Christ evolved to where our vibrations were vibrating so quickly that we could do as Christ and walk on water? I feel with my entire being that this is possible, it takes one becoming more than oneself, it takes that connection with the omnipotent, it's an immersion of the spirit in heaven while on earth, and more sacrifices than most are willing to make, including myself. The question begs, "Why aren't we willing to make the sacrifices that will bring us to heaven while still on the earthly plane?" The spirit is willing but the flesh is weak. Isn't the sacrifice worth it?*

We perceive the sacrifice as to much, though we realize the reward will come later, we cannot really perceive ourselves in heaven reaping the rewards of a life well lived, although we know from books and movies, what others have envisioned how heaven would look, however putting your soul in position to make highly evolved sacrifices is completely different and a very noble place to live life. I know that one is on Earth a miniscule amount of time, and in heaven an eternity.

Chapter 10

Soul Mates

While we are making all of these sacrifices we are to be walking with our Twin Soul or our Soul Mate. God in his infinite wisdom created a partner for each of us and it is up to God to move us into position so we locate our other half. Twins are an example of a Twin Soul, you are cut from the same spiritual fabric, an as with twins, they miss their siblings when they are apart from them, we long for our Twin or Soul mate throughout our life journey, we realize something fundamental is missing in our lives, though we have God but not our other half, so we search and search endlessly, desiring to find our twin soul or mate. Genesis 2:18 "In the Garden of Eden, God said, "It is not good that man should be alone," and he made a help meet for him."

Have you ever dreamed of finding your soul mate? Of course you have. Have you wondered if you would you know him if you saw him? When I was 22, I found my soul mate. A man to whom I was completely in sync with; which made our connection truly profound. When I say profound, I mean that our souls actually recognized each other. I saw him first, he did not see me. I was of course in a nightclub with some of my girlfriends when I saw him, he was beautiful. He was the most beautiful man that I had ever seen. When I saw him, I thought that he was probably very vain because how could you not be, when you are beautiful in the eyes of the world. After I got to know him better and introduced him around to family and friends, one of my girlfriends described him as a Greek god. The outer man was 5'11" tall, with beautiful curly brown hair, a cleft in his chin, brown almond shaped eyes, and

119

generous lips, not too generous but what one would find sensuous and high cheek bones. He was a beautiful man on the outside and also on the inside. I could tell immediately that he was beautiful on the outside just by looking at him; once I got to know him I found that he also had a beautiful spirit, the beauty on the outside could not hold a light to the beauty of the inner man.

When I first saw him, I told my girlfriends I was going to meet him, and they looked at me in disbelief. I just knew that I had to meet him. I told my girlfriends that I was going to walk up to him and say, "Haven't we met somewhere before?" My girlfriends giggled because they felt that I would get some type of set down as response to that question. But truthfully, haven't you seen someone, or met someone who you thought perhaps you had met somewhere before but just couldn't put your finger on where you had met? (It could be a male or female, and then when you met, it seemed as if you had known this person forever, there was an automatic connection.) Of course my friends thought I was crazy, maybe I was, I just knew I had to meet him. I recognized him, I knew it was a line but somewhere in my mind, I did recognize him. I knew him from somewhere, but I didn't know where I had previously met him, or maybe I hadn't met him. But the thing about it was, he thought he knew me also and he couldn't figure out where he knew me from either.

Looking back on it, some things are much clearer than they were at the time of the meeting. After I went up and met him my friends were of course in awe, he was by far the best looking man in the club. His name was Christopher; after he left my life, I was to encounter many more men named Chris, or some derivative there of. It wasn't because I was consciously looking for him, but unconsciously, I looked for him in every man I met and under every rock. It still brings a lump to my throat to think about him.

He was in the military and we began an intense relationship,

I saw him every day and night. We were so close that when we made love it was as though our spirits actually joined. This type of lovemaking is definitely otherworldly. It was if our spirits actually rose out of our bodies and intertwined, and actually became one spirit. The spirits were neither him, nor I, but US, because in those moments we were truly one. We enjoyed each other's company and got along very well. This seems like a simple statement, but it is very difficult at times to get along with men and not swallow your pride and back down from what's on the tip of your tongue to respond to your significant other. But with Chris it was easy; it was an easy non-stressful beautiful relationship. It was every woman's dream of the relationship that you will have for the rest of your life. It wouldn't matter if you were rich or poor, as long as you could be with your mate. You would go to the ends of earth to ensure that this relationship remained together. We grew very close, so close that after he was deployed to Guam, I had dreams about him. I believe because we were so connected that I could feel, or perceive what was going on with him if it was going to cause him danger.

By the time the military deployed Chris to Guam we had planned to marry when he returned. I will never forget my last moments with Chris; a friend of his had a dinner for the girlfriends and wives they were leaving behind. I don't remember what we had for dinner; I do remember getting lost trying to find our way to his friend's house. He was a typical male, who did not want to stop and get directions; we eventually found his friend's home after we stopped for directions.

I do remember that we left his friend's house and went back home, we only had a few hours together before I had to take him to the base to catch the bus, which would take the guys to the plane. This was at the military base, Pt. Hueneme. I never considered that there would be a bus to take the guys to the plane that they were actually going to fly out on, but there were many men leaving at this time, so they loaded them all on a bus. I also remember when he left me and got on, and this is the irony, a yellow bus. I could see him from the window of the bus. He blew me kisses from the bus as it took off.

I still remember it as if it were only yesterday, something told me to hold onto this memory as if it would be the last look that I would have of him. And it was exactly that, the last look I had of him.

I thought to my self that this is irrational, he was not going into a war situation, he was just going to an Island and after he did his tour of nine months he would return.

That did not happen, as it should have. I remember writing to him everyday, believe it or not, because I couldn't believe that I was writing him every day at the time. Looking back, it is hard for me to believe that I wrote to him every day. He sent me tapes that he recorded instead of writing to me. I really appreciated hearing his voice and hearing everything that he was thinking while he was gone.

His mother was from Germany with a very heavy German accent, while he was in Guam, we spoke to one another. Christopher's father was African American and had instilled in him that he was also African American, he told me his father told him he had no choice, in terms of picking his ethnicity, although his mother was German. He would always be perceived as African American because of the color of his skin. His father ground in him the realities of living as an African American man in the United States. When he left we missed each other desperately.

Chapter 11

The Dreams

Christopher would call me from Guam; the government had a Watts line which he could use to call me from time to time. I remember after one conversation with him feeling that he was not safe where he was located. He had mentioned to me that the Guamanian's did not like the military men, especially the men native to Guam. The women in Guam were attracted to the military men, in hopes of marrying and getting off of the Island. The conversation Christopher and I had was disturbing to me, my spirit felt somewhat unsettled. That night when I went to bed, I dreamed that someone took me by my hand, a (spirit) and as we floated I was led to this beautiful Island that was lush and green. There were all types of tropical plants there along with beautiful wild flowers. As I hovered above the Island, there was a scene which unfolded beneath me. I saw Christopher and two other men. Christopher had his hands tied behind his back, and the two men held huge machete's in their hands. Christopher was telling his captors that he would basically what ever they wanted if they would release him. Christopher was smiling and joking as he stated in a nonchalant manner "Guys, it will not do you any good to kill me; you still won't have what you want." In the dream I did not pay much attention to the woman, other than the fact that she was a captive along with Christopher. For whatever reason, Christopher was not taking the situation seriously. That became his downfall. He said "look here man, I don't know what happened to the rest of the Ganja, but there is more where that came from, if you kill me you won't get the rest of the Ganja or your money." The captors told Christopher and the woman to turn around and take off their shirts, at this point Christopher became more serious however, he still did not believe he was about to be killed. The men came from behind Christopher and the woman, and before they knew what was happening to them, they were stabbed in the back. As I hovered above the scene, I tried to go down to where Christopher was so that I could warn him about what was happening, especially regarding the machetes. But I couldn't, no matter how hard I tried I couldn't warn him, so there before my very eyes I witnessed Christopher get stabbed to death and there was nothing that I could do to prevent his death from taking place.

I woke up from my dream/nightmare and went straight to my sister's room. We were room mates at the time and many times after this; I knocked on the door of her room, and asked her to get up and pray with me. I was in tears, I told her that I had witnessed Christopher getting killed, and tears streamed down my face the entire time I told her that I needed her to pray with me. I told her that we needed to pray that Christopher was guided and protected while he was in Guam. We prayed the normal prayer, "Father in the name of Jesus protect and guide Christopher while he is in Guam." There was a lot more the prayer but it went along those lines.

I felt comforted that my sister and I prayed together for Christopher; however I felt I still needed to do more. Which is always the case for me? I wish that I could just let things be without having to do more to ensure that matters were really O.K. So therefore, I wired him, all I wired was, "Call me, it's important. Love, Vanda."

Well within a day or two I received my phone call from Christopher, and I told him to be careful. I said, "I don't know what you are doing, but you need to be careful." He responded jokingly, "I'm just trying to make a little money honey, so that when I get home we can get married." And of course, because I knew this was, a no nonsense matter, my response was, "The money will make no difference what so ever, if you never make it home." His response was "Don't worry; I've got it all under control."

Chapter 12

The Dream Becomes a Nightmare

Now at this juncture you are probably wondering, why I didn't tell him what I had dreamed. The closest I came to telling him was "the money will make no difference if you don't make it home." I don't exactly know why I didn't tell him what I had dreamed. However upon revisiting the dream and what took place, during the dream I tried to warn him and that was to no avail, perhaps this was to signify that no matter how hard I tried I would be unable to get him to change his course. Maybe it had to do with my inability to contact him while I watched the scene being played out in front of my eyes, I don't know. I kicked myself, and blamed myself hundreds of times for not telling him about my dream. I thought to myself after he had been killed, if I would have warned him, would things still have turned out the same? I guess over the years, I have determined that when it is your time to go, you will go.

Well I dreamed this dream two more times, with less intensity each time I dreamed it. The last time I dreamt this dream, I went to my aunt Glen, who is a very spiritual woman, and she had the ability to interpret dreams and prophesy. When I told her of the dreams that I had dreamt, she stated that "sometimes we dream these dreams and they don't mean anything." So I was comforted by this notion, because prior to my conversation with my aunt I was walking around with a heavy heart, so I released the death warnings. This means I released them to the Father.

One day, as I sat in my mother's den the phone rang, and somehow I knew that it was bad news, but I sat on the sofa and didn't move. It's like all of a sudden your heart feels heavy for no reason what so ever, the tempo of your heart speeds up, you feel as though you are barely breathing at all, because now you are taking very shallow breaths in dread of what's coming next. And the thing is you are not completely sure of what you are dreading, but somewhere in the recesses of your mind, the name "CHRISTOPHER" rings out. Then all of a sudden instead of taking shallow breaths you stop breathing waiting for what you know, but don't want to know, and will not accept.

When my mother told me that the call was for me, my heart plummeted, a feeling of actual pain encompassed my heart. I moved from the sofa to the floor to take the call, the man on the phone told me his name; (Daryl or Toney, I'm not sure, I couldn't remember his name right after he told me what it was), I had no recollection of who he was and I still cannot remember what he told me his name was. He began describing to me where he met me; he was at the dinner before Christopher had left for Guam. I still did not recognize who he was so I said "yeah, yeah," I just wanted him to get on with what he had called to tell me. And then he said it, "I'm sorry to tell you this but Christopher is no longer with us." (I continue to remember those exact words to this day.)

And of course I became hysterical, I shouted, "what do you mean he is no longer with us?" I knew exactly what he meant but, my mind refused to believe what he said. I knew in my soul that this was true, but I refused to really believe him. Even after I had dreamed that he was killed, I still did not want to believe what he was saying was true. I was rude to him, I told him "I don't know who you are, but this is not funny!" The mind is a magnificent part of our bodies, it controls and regulates everything, our bodily functions, our perceptions everything.

I am finding while writing this, I am experiencing the same type of pain I experienced during the time when the event occurred. I have taken a three-month hiatus from the book because some experiences feel like opening up old wounds. I realize that Christopher is still close whenever I need him, but the loss of him still brings me to tears and pain to my heart, even after twenty-two years.

This morning I woke up to the call of the lord, I felt that the lord was directing and telling me that I was one of the enlightened ones and also that my mother was one. Now this does not infer or imply that others within my family structure are not enlightened, but I was born to my mother because of her gifts and her ability to motivate me to write this book.

Honestly, I could not believe Christopher was dead. I remember my mother taking the phone from me and asking the person on the phone to indicate who he was, and after about 10 minutes she slowly hung up the phone. My mother came to me and held me in her arms as I sobbed in shock and disbelief, and rocked me like a baby, instead of the twenty-two year old I was, as tears poured from my eyes and down my face like the torrents of a waterfall. I cried and I cried, I was hysterical, my mother had to give me some valium to calm me down, but I was inconsolable. I continued to cry, and then, I heard Christopher speaking to me, how I knew it was Christopher I cannot tell you, but I knew it was him. "What's wrong baby, don't cry. I know that you are not crying because of me, there is no reason to cry." Believe it or not, I sopped crying. I believe that Christopher did not immediately know that he was dead: he was murdered execution style. How do I know this, well there are reports from people who have died suddenly and come back have stated, that they did not know that they had died.

The people responsible for his death, as I stated previously made him take off his shirt along the woman who he was with, they were ordered to turn around and they shot them in the back.

It was like the movie the *Onion Fields*, which was the impression I received. It was not exactly like the dream, but very similar.

I had waited eight months for Christopher to return home, and he was to come home the next month. His death occurred on approximately April 28th. The military is not exactly sure of the date of his death because it took them a few days to find the bodies, because of the lush green foliage. I remember the date the military stated that he died because he was only days away from his twenty-first birthday, which was May 14th.

Yet, I still could not believe that he was dead, everywhere I went, I saw someone who looked like him, but it was not him. I wired his Chaplin in the military, because I refused to believe that he was not coming home, God I loved him so much, so much that at one point, I believed God was punishing me for putting a man before him, later I realized that I was not being punished, but that Christopher's death was just something that I needed to go through in order to refine my soul so that one day I could be with God.

The loss of a loved one, stretches your soul through your endurance you are able to grow spiritually in a manner that would have taken years to reach, these are spiritual growing pains. Whenever any event in your life touches you as completely and profoundly as the loss of a child, lover or family member your soul has to stretch in order to survive and completely understand and comprehend the event that has taken place. At times like these you question the nature of life and its relevance. Questions like, why are we born? Or are we born just to die? Is there a purpose for me in this life? What type of job should I have in order to do God's will? You also question God. "Why did God let this happen, why wasn't God there to watch over my loved one, isn't he supposed to be there? Also," I keep all the commandments, and do good works aren't my loved ones and I supposed to be covered by the blood of the lamb?" You have learned in Sunday school that "God's got the whole world in his hands."

And so now you believe that God has let you down and forsaken you by not preventing your loss. Perhaps your loss had to take place because God is doing what has been stated in the Bible, "That he has prepared a place for you in his kingdom." Your soul must be refined enough in order for you to see his kingdom. John 14:2-3

> In my Father's house are many mansions;
> If it were not so,
> I would have told you.
> I go and prepare a place for you.
> 3And if I go prepare a place for you,
> I will come again and receive you to Myself'
> That where I am,
> There you may be also.

Christopher was a good soul, just like Aleejha the pop music singer, she died in a plane crash, needlessly, and reportedly she was just as beautiful on the inside as she was on the outside.

Events such as this test our souls, sometimes we wonder why God let these types of events take place, or we just blame God. But if we believe, and have faith, we will come to realize that "everything under the sun, takes place for a purpose," although during our time of grief we can't see or understand that there is a reason and purpose.

Chapter 13

Emotional Amnesia

After Christopher's death, I was depressed for at least three years, the summer after he passed; I was preparing to attend the University of California, Santa Barbara. My first year there, I found that I could not write, my thoughts were blocked and confused, this was amazing to me because writing had always been something that I was very good at doing. But I could not write, I didn't understand what was happening to me. After doing poorly on a few essay exams, I discussed my problems with another student (T.A. teacher's assistant) whose major was psychology.

As I began to describe the events of my recent past, (six months prior to attending the university) he told me that I was angry with Christopher. Of course, I questioned his logic, how could I be angry with someone who was the victim of circumstances? The Teacher's.Assistant, put it into perspective for me, he stated that, "I was angry with Christopher for leaving me, it did not matter that he was the victim, all of my dreams had been shattered." (This was true; Christopher had asked me to marry him and I had waited for him while he was away). I remember laying in my bed at night sobbing and asking Christopher how he could do this to me, "How could you leave me after it took so long to find you, my soul mate?" How many nights I cried, and sobbed and became angry, I do not know. It's just that when you feel that your heart is wrenched out of your chest, and the pain is excruciating, it is unbearable but you have to bear the pain anyway, because there are people within your family that love you and count on your presence because they love you. I now really understand the play by Shakespeare "Romeo and Juliet" when you love someone to that depth and magnitude, the thought may occur to you to leave (commit suicide) in order to not live without your mate because perhaps you can meet them on the other side. However suicide is a deadly sin. You have to stay here on this earthly plane, which is something that you chose even before you were born, to walk the path that you are now walking. You did not necessarily chose to come and walk without your soul mate beside you, but you chose to encounter your soul mate, and his or her choices were for them to make. Often times we don't see the whole picture when we are making life changing choices, we don't realize that these are life changing choices that we are making and therefore we make the decision we feel is best at the time. It often just seems the right thing to do at that time.

Looking back on these events, I realize how selfish I was being; however there was little that I could do about feeling abandoned by Christopher. It brought back memories of abandonment by my father as a child of five. My entire life has been impacted by my feelings of abandonment stemming from events resulting from an alcoholic father. I don't know if my father's alcoholism had anything to do with his treatment of my sister and myself. I remember one incident which is a primary example of why the abandonment by Christopher, resulted in a life changing event.

One morning about two or three in the morning, my sister began to cry. My sister at this time was 2 years old, I was 5 years old. I ushered my sister out to stand in front of the door of my parent's bedroom while she cried. I had tried to console her but what I did, didn't work, and what does a 5 year old know about consoling a 2 year old. Of course my father came out of his room, highly annoyed and also wanted to know what problem my baby sister was having. She basically said she was afraid so he took her in his arms and held her gently and took her into my parent's room. I of course tried to follow, only to be shouted at and told to go back to bed, my father said, and "You are too big and too old to sleep in your parent's bedroom." I could don't ever remember being permitted to sleep in my parent's bedroom. The door was shut in my face, no hug, no kiss good night, no explanation, except that I was too old to go in my parent's room and that my sister was only a baby. My mother came into my bedroom to console me because she had heard the exchange, but somehow because she was not my father, I was not consoled.

Keep in mind, at 5 years old, I could not process being too old to be held and hugged, and to this day, I still can't process that. But picture this, my father taking my little sister into their room, and a little 5 year old standing by the door heart broken, because she somehow always knew he didn't really love her. I ran back to my room and threw myself on my bed and sobbed uncontrollably. These hurts from early childhood have a tendency to replay themselves time and time again.

So when Christopher my soul-mate, he truly was, and I had to go through many frogs before I found him, a part of me died that had shut down as a child, which had opened up to love Christopher, shut down. We do all types of things to protect ourselves from hurts and perceived hurts.

The T.A. told me to state what it was that I was angry about, and to tell Christopher, of course another waterfall began, and I told Christopher all of the reasons that I was angry with him; most of all was the abandonment. And in years to come I would tell Christopher "I can't believe that you left me," time and time again. I had warned Christopher, to be careful but he did not take heed; but what can you do when certain events are already set in motion?

After Christopher's, death there was a sighting of Christopher; my baby brother Weldon, had seen a man running in and out of the closet, where we had stored Christopher's clothing. He had been seen on more than one occasion and there was no man in the house fitting his description.

Two months after Christopher's death, his battalion returned to Port Hueneme, MCB9. The guys he went to Guam with returned to Oxnard. The most interesting of his friends were Jasper and Jasper. Both of these men looked similar to Christopher, especially Jasper. Both Jasper and Jasper came to see me when they returned to convey their condolences. Jasper, I had met before he went to Guam, Jasper I hadn't met.

Of course I had questions that I wanted answered regarding Christopher's death. I asked Jasper, "Describe exactly how Christopher died." Jasper told me that he believed that "Christopher had been set up, that his death was a case of mistaken identify, it was Jasper they were looking for." Jasper said that Christopher and Jasper had been friends and that they were both selling marijuana in Guam. Christopher had set up a drug deal and Jasper had been purchasing marijuana for Christopher. Jasper had shorted Christopher and he did not have the agreed upon amount of marijuana to sell when he went to make the exchange. Jasper stated that he felt that Christopher had been set up and that the Guamanians were really looking for Jasper not Christopher because Jasper had sold to them previously. Jasper and Christopher did look similar and that would be an easy mistake to make, and this would make my dream make sense because in the dream Christopher, was stabbed in the back; (reality shot)

Needless to say that after Christopher had died; a part of my spirit seemed to die for a while. It took at least three years before I could discuss Chris's death without breaking down into tears. I remember encountering a woman on my job at the County office, where I worked as a student worker; the county employed me through my work-study funds from the local Jr. College. I worked in the County Surveyor's office where I was a glorified clerk. You really never understand how the influence of one of life's decisions can lead you into future jobs. In the County Surveyor's Office, I Xeroxed the Engineers work, run blue-line copies of Engineers drawings.

Chapter 14

The Lady in Black

One day when I was taking my break, in the break room, a woman came up to me and asked if she could sit at the table with me. I'm a loner, but I am never rude and I'm not sure if there was other seating or not, however I grudgingly acquiesced to her request. I've noticed in my life, that although I always do the right thing there are times when I don't do it in the proper spirit. Meaning, I would have rather sat alone so I could be left with my thoughts and my pain.

I don't remember this woman's name but I am sure she was guided to sit with me through divine guidance. I of course was reading a book, which is what I always do especially when you are in a place with a number of people and you have no one to sit with you. (Probably some romance novel which is what I read in those days.) This lady looked somewhat drawn and very pale; she had kind eyes and a nice smile. She began to talk about God. She asked me if I was a Christian. I said "yes". She asked "what denomination do you belong to?" I replied "Pentecostal, Baptist, we all believe the same and basically worship in the same way. However the Pentecostal are much stricter than the Baptist." She began to tell me her story. Before she began to tell me her story she asked me what I was doing at the Government Center (County Offices). I stated that I was a work-study student, and I was working as a clerk at the County Surveyor's office, running Blue lines and Xeroxing copies for the Engineers. Of course she wanted to know where I was attending college and what I wanted to become. I stated "I am studying *Criminal Law and Society*" in order to become an attorney." That is when she launched into her story. She replied "My husband was in a major accident, and we had to hire attorneys to work for us. That is when we found out how crooked lawyers are." She went on to state that the attorneys basically sold her and her husband out. That they, (the attorneys), got together and decided how they needed to play the game, so that they would come out with the majority of capital. The attorneys made these closed door bargains which ended up costing her and her husband all of their money. She said, "This is not the field that you want to get into because the attorneys are crooked and are out for them selves. They sell their clients out and do whatever it takes to make a profit." She stated, that she could tell that I was a spiritual person and perhaps I should consider something like teaching. (I thought to myself, I wonder if she knows my mother is a professor at Ventura College. Of course she didn't) The Lady in Black, as I will refer to her from here on, asked me if I knew how to pray? I said of course, I know how to pray. That is one of the first things that you are taught in many African American households. She said, "Tell me how you pray." And of course I fell back on "Our father, who art in Heaven. Her response was, "Is that it?" I said "well mostly, unless there is something that I really want or need, then after I say the Lord's Prayer, I'll add on my needs as an addendum." (Which is what I continue to do to this day)? She continued by stating "That while I prayed, I should be talking to God, just like I was having a conversation with anyone else." I said "oh." Then she asked an amazing question, "Does God talk to you?" Well I was twenty-two years old, and knew nothing of even the possibility of God (lowering himself off of his throne) to talk to me. Of course one of my thoughts was, "who am I to believe that God would talk to me?" The Lady In Black's response to my **No** comment was, "He will you know." "He will what, I replied" "Talk to you" said the Lady in Black. I replied, "Why would God talk to me, he has enough to keep him busy. And who am I to try to gain God's attention?"

I couldn't wait until I could take a break and employ what the woman in Black had told me. I went into the women's break room, which was the women's lounge, it contained an avocado leather sofa and a couple of leather arm chairs. There was not much traffic; I took my break at a time when I felt most people had already taken their break.

I sat there reviewing what the woman in Black had told me about talking to God and having God talk to me. I didn't know if it would work, but I was going to try and see what would happen. I sat and meditated thinking of God and his goodness. I felt that I was a very blessed person in that I had a home, a job and working on becoming more educated; I was on my way to the University of California in Santa Barbara in the fall. I thanked the lord as the Lady in Black had instructed and then I sat quietly waiting for God to talk to me.

All of the sudden a voice entered into my mind, a still quiet, calm voice, and the voice which I have come to know as the voice of the Lord God. "Why should I speak in a loud booming voice, when I can talk to you quietly in the recesses of your mind, there is no reason for everyone to know what it is that I say to you." And as I sat in the women's lounge having my conversation with the Lord God, I marveled at what was taking place while it was taking place. I am at work talking to God and the awesome thing about that was that God was talking to me. I was told to do some very significant things which would bring peace to me and others at the same time. I had to go and apologize to several people who I had wronged, intentionally and unintentionally.

Chapter 15

The Apologies

First I had to apologize to my sister. Because of what was previously discussed I needed to give her a heart felt apology and really work on being nicer to her. It was not her fault that my father had used her to get back at me because I did not like him. I told her that I was sorry for everything that I had said and done to her which had hurt her feelings. My sister, had a very peaceful and calm demeanor, she smiled and said "that's o.k." I knew that she appreciated my apology, and although it made her feel better and she forgave me, it was not o.k. What my apology did was open up channels of communication between my sister and me. We hugged each other and shed a few tears because of the years of hurt feelings that were to tender to even discuss. There were many occasions where we hurt each other, better yet when I hurt my sister, such as the time when, I slapped my sister's face, for sneaking and wearing my clothes. I never perceived it as though she wanted to be like me, I always felt that she was wearing my clothes just to annoy me. Upon retrospect, she did want to wear my clothes to be more like me, because I was her older sister, and even though I was mean to her, she loved me in spite of myself. Our being raised in a Pentecostal church, laid the foundation for us forgiving others.

The other person I had to apologize to was a girlfriend of mine. I was to find out later in life that the situation that I went through with my girlfriend over a man would be repeated on several occasions until I was able to respond to the situation in a Godly manner. The situation with my girlfriend, Pearlie, was that the guy she went out with asked me out after they had broken up.

And being her girlfriend I was privy to her personal information regarding her ex-boyfriend. I have to admit that I liked him also being 22 years old having very little relationship experience, I was not exactly sure of how I was to respond in this relationship regarding Pearlie's ex-boyfriend when he asked me out. I knew that they were not going out any longer, but what I did not know was that she still cared about him. However in reflection, I don't think I cared enough to find out if she was still into him. She had already told me that they were not together; I should have taken it a step further to find out if she was still into him. When I began to date Pearlie's ex-boy friend, I found out through her tears and feelings of betrayal how she felt about him.

Chapter 16

Fast for 7 days and 7 nights

I began to attend church more often after my experience with the Woman In Black, God had also told me, besides apologizing to fast for 7 days and 7 nights. One evening after attending a very spirit filled church service and during my fast, where I became filled with the Holy Spirit and spoke in tongues; I returned home feeling blessed. I parked the car across the street from the house, at that time I was driving Christopher's car, he had left it with me when he went to Guam. I got out of the car, it was night, but the street lights were on and I was lived in a safe neighborhood, I closed and locked the door to the car. As I began to cross the street there were whispers loud enough for me to hear, "Hey, hey," I looked around and I did not see anyone. As I proceeded to walk, I heard the whisper again, "Hey, hey, over hear, over hear!" I said "What, who is that?" I looked down the street; I tried to see behind the parked cars, there was no one there. I bent over, squatted down, tried to look under cars to see if there was anyone, there was no one. So when the voice whispered out again, and by this time I was getting a little frightened, I did what I was taught to do in church. I stated very loud and clear "Satan the lord rebukes you! In the name of Jesus." And I never heard that whispers of the voices again. I feel that when you become filled with the Holy Spirit you vibrate at a different rate and you can become vulnerable to spirits, as Jesus did after he fasted for 40days and 40 nights. My attending church did give me the wherewithal to withstand verbal attacks after graduating from college and to also learn the lesson to be learned at that stage of my journey.

Chapter 17

Internship in Washington DC

I wish that this was the only instance when I and a girlfriend came into conflict over a man, but it was not. I will say, that although the next couple of times I did not get my response completely correct, however I did better than the first time. I guess part of my problem was that I could not understand why the man would choose me over my girlfriend. I was always reticent, never forward and yet they would choose me, which invariably caused problems between me and my girlfriends. Even when the guy would state, can't I chose the person I would like to date? One girlfriend, Chastity, went straight off, the fire hit the fan.

Chastity and I went to Washington D.C. after we had completed the University of California in Santa Barbara. We had hung out as undergraduate students, taken some of the same classes together; we were both movers and shakers. I became the President Of the "Black Student Union" as it was known in those days and she was the vice President. She was going to school to become a programmer; I didn't know what I was going to school to become. Initially I felt that I might become an attorney however I felt that I needed to speak to more attorneys and determine whether they felt their job was gratifying /rewarding.

Chastity and I worked on a research project that was presented in Washington D.C. to determine why the University was unable to graduate a significant number of African American students after matriculation to the University. The bottom line was that the students felt alienated at the University, often they had Caucasian room mates and the cultural differences presented their own problems.

A graduate student took our research to Capital Hill and presented it to the Department of Education in Washington D.C. Although we received very little credit for the research we were able to add it to our resumes when we applied for internships in Washington D.C. We were both awarded Fellowships which would cover our room and board for the summer in D.C. Now how exciting was this. The internships began before we were able to march and receive our diplomas for our Bachelor's degrees, therefore neither of us marched, and we headed straight to D.C. and our apartment which was close to Rock Creek Park, (The Woodener). Chastity and I were both returning students which meant that we attended the university as unmarried students with children in tow. I had a six year old daughter and she had a twelve year old son. We both sent our children to stay with relatives so that we would be able to take advantage of this opportunity. I sent my daughter to stay with her father and Chastity sent her son to stay with her Mother.

We were very excited, I remember our first day at our new home, Chastity wanted to go walking in our surrounding neighborhood. I said o.k. I was game to explore our new environment. It was a beautiful sunny June day in D.C., I was 27 and Chastity was 32 we both looked young. We had great figures, I was 34. 24, 34 and Chastity was 32, 24, 36. Of course we attracted attention as we walked through the neighborhood. The homes were very nice, with well manicured lawns. There happened to be a couple of men outside washing their cars as we passed. They called out to us; Chastity responded and crossed the street. I waited for her because I was not interested at that point in time. We were going to begin our new internships in a couple of days and that was first and foremost on my mind. Working for the Peace Corps as an intern made me feel as though I was contributing to society as I helped myself. Chastity was interning with the newly formed Black Entertainment Network.

When Chastity returned she stated that the two guys wanted us to cook them dinner. Cooking was never my thing and I told her that I did not want to go over to a couple of strange guys house to cook for them, no matter how good looking they were, and they were gorgeous, and of course there was one who was better looking than the other. After we returned to our room Chastity told me that she wanted the best looking one, Lucas. Of course I said O.K., I didn't know them and was not planning to get to know them. That's when she told me that she had Lucas and his friend that we would come over to their homes the following day to cook. I told Chastity "I can't and I don't cook." She responded that's O.K. I'll cook; I cook well enough for both of us.

I felt that it was an imposition for her to agree for me that I was going to go over to these guys house to cook. I would find in life that this was another pattern that would repeat itself when I did not stand up for what I wanted. I told Chastity "You can go over there and cook for them but I am not." She responded, "Please, I can't go over there by myself. I'll do all the cooking; all you have to do is to go with me." Well of course I couldn't let her go over there by herself, so reluctantly I agreed.

The following day we went over to Lucas's house, where he lived with his two other male roommates. It was filthy, Chastity and I went into the kitchen and we looked at each other because the dishes had not been washed for about a week. Chastity told the guys that the kitchen needed to be cleaned before she could cook, Lucas volunteered, and Chastity said that she would help him. I told Chastity, "Don't look at me, this was not my idea." I went into the living room while Chastity and Lucas cleaned the kitchen and Chastity cooked.

I was speaking with the other roommates when Lucas came over to me and handed me a piece of paper. We were standing in the living room and Chastity was working in the kitchen. He said "call me, maybe we can go out sometime." I looked at the paper; it had all of his contact information on it. I said, "Chastity likes you. She will be upset if she knew that you gave me this paper. She has already claimed you, so it doesn't matter how I feel." Lucas responded, "I met you both at the same time." I stated, "But you don't get it, she set this whole thing up so she could get to know you better. She even cleaned your kitchen and cooked for you. I don't want to take this paper from you. This is going to really piss her off. I tried to give the paper back to Lucas." Lucas's response was, "I know, but I like you. Don't I get to chose?" My response was "She is going to be really mad." At the time I didn't realize how angry she would become.

After we returned to our room Chastity was fuming. She knew that Lucas had given me his information. I tried to talk to her and tell her that I had told Lucas that she liked him. I told her that I had tried to give him his information back, and he wouldn't take it. I also told her that I had told him that she had liked him. She didn't care. She ranted and raved about how I was flirting with him even though I didn't say a word to him. He had invited me to help him with the kitchen, when Chastity had volunteered, I turned him down. I reminded Chastity of that and she continued to rant and rave about my nonverbal flirting.

I had to consider what she was stating; honestly I did not consciously or unconsciously flirt with Lucas. I stayed away from him, and barely even spoke to him. I tried to hand Chastity Lucas's information, she shrugged the slip of paper off and said "keep it, he gave it to you." I said O.K.

Lucas was 5'10', about 160 lbs with an olive completion and straight coal black hair. You could barley tell that he was an African

American, I found in D.C. that there were many quadroons and octoroons who claimed to be African American but were not visibly African American.

With this situation with Chastity, which actually repeated itself twice, I feel that I responded appropriately. In the end I asked her if she would mind if I dated Lucas, of course she did, but said that she didn't mind.

After you have had similar scenarios play themselves out in your life, you must question what it is you were to learn from this event. And when the event repeats itself the question must be asked, did you learn what you should have learned from this event. The event with Lucas and Chastity, I should not have taken his information because it hurt Chastity. Although I did nothing to solicit a relationship with Lucas, I should have sacrificed this potential relationship, even though I was completely honest with Chastity and Lucas, Chastity felt betrayed.

Although Lucas and I never consummated a relationship, even when he came to California, I liked him enough to have a relationship with him; however there are times when one has to make sacrifices because of past misdeeds. You may not even realize that there was in the past that you did that was not morally correct however you continuously encounter the same set of basic circumstances, and for some reason the relationship just doesn't work out.

During the time I lived in Washington D.C. and worked for the Peace Corps, along with a short stint with the National Organization for Women, which I was told after having been hired there was full of lesbians; which I did not believe. However, I found out that it was basically the truth, after overhearing conversations regarding members who were lesbians and the parties they attended. I was shocked, but at that point in time, I was waiting on a permanent position to come through with the Peace Corps, my Internship had been completed, and I needed the job as an Account Receivables Clerk. The Permanent position did come through with the Peace Corps but it took at least 2-3 months before I was hired as an employee after I had completed my internship.

I enjoyed living in Washington D.C., it was a completely different environment than living in California; I enjoyed the free concerts in Rock Creek Park, and the enthusiasm for living that many of the inhabitants shared. One of the main reasons that I remained in D.C. after the completion of the internship was because of Ivan Williams.

I have a cousin that lives in D.C., she agreed to put me up until I found a job and could get an apartment of my own, which was very kind of her seeing that she had three children of her own. I was able to move into an apartment with a girl who worked for the National Organization of Women, she found out that I was looking for a room and offered me one in her Condo. Initially I thought this was a great idea, after moving in with Susan, I found out that she was controlling and on drugs.

Personally, I have always thought that I looked O.K., but the way women respond to me regarding their boyfriends escapes me. Her boyfriend came over one night to visit, I stayed in my room, only passing through the area where her and her boyfriend were for water, she stopped and introduced me to him and I proceeded to my room.

The next thing I knew she was ranting and raving about how I had flirted with her boyfriend, (I only told him my name) and she went off on me. She literally went off on me, she followed me out of my room to the restroom, ranting and raving about how I had wasted her water when I showered, that there was always water on the floor in the bathroom. Of course I apologized, this incensed her more, and I moved back into the bedroom. She followed me into the bedroom, by that time she had picked up a screw driver on the way; she shook it at me and stated "You had better get your ass out of my house before I stab you with this screw driver." She said this in front of her 5 year old daughter.

I immediately picked up the phone and called my cousin and told her that she needed to pick me up right away. I don't even think I spent two nights at her Condo. My cousin came with her daughter and gave Berlinda a look of "I dare you to mess with my cousin." That was that, however I still remained in D.C. and over the course of a year I dated Ivan.

There were some things about Ivan that I liked, others that I did not like, especially the fact that he could have lightened my load by sharing an apartment with me, but wouldn't. He would not commit to anything, and the thing that I disliked most about him was that, when we began to date he insinuated that he had one child, five months later I found out that he had three children. Now that was not the only problem I had with him, he was 30 years old and still living at home. We had some major cultural differences because from my perspective there is a point to which you need to get out on your own and stop living with your mother and father.

Although, I loved Ivan, I moved back to California because he was not the type of man that I would respect, nor trust completely. There were times when he was supposed to show up at my apartment for the weekend, no call, nothing, he just would not show up, I loved him. I would spend the entire weekend crying waiting on him, and then on Sunday evening he might show up saying that he went to New Jersey to visit his daughter. Now that is all good and fine, but knowing what my situation is, along with proper etiquette, a phone call goes a long way. Too many times I trusted him and he killed my heart, thereby killing the chances of us having a significant relationship. He can be my friend, but that's it, I can never say never, because never has a tendency of coming back to bite you in the, you know where.

Chapter 18

"Eternal Sunshine in the Spotless Mind"

It is like playing a video over and over again, similar to "Eternal Sunshine In the Spotless Mind" which has several different endings except this movie is real life, and the ending you create either helps you move closer to the almighty, or not move at all in terms of furthering your spiritual evolution or move further away from the father, which slows your spiritual progress.

Most of the time while we are traveling through life, we are unaware of why we are here on earth. However if you are a person who is in tune to spirituality and the purpose for your journey you can make great gains in your spiritual growth. In the process you can also help others see their purpose for being here on earth right now during this time period.

Chapter 19

The Legacy

Grandma Higgins and Grandpa Higgins were my great, great grand parents, and they passed on a legacy of teaching and Christianity. Grandma Higgins was 12 years old when she was released from slavery, her Masters did not mistreat her and she was taught to read and write. She was mixed as were most African Americans, the mix was African and Cherokee. She married Grandpa Higgins who also knew how to read and write, which was a skill which they loved sharing. My great, great grandparents knew the journey (path) that they had to take, they did it freely with spiritual enthusiasm because their connection to the father was so great that they knew the lord would protect them. Grandma and Grandpa Higgins lived in Mississippi, during the 1860s, prior to 1865 it was illegal to teach blacks to read and write. However my great grandparents felt that it was what they were here to do, it was a part of their spiritual evolution to face odds and teach other African Americans to read and write.

In Mississippi my great, great grandparents were harassed to the extent that they had to quickly leave Mississippi or face death. But from their perspective, God being God, and being good, would move them to another area where they could continue on their path. Unfortunately when they were ran out of Mississippi they had to leave one of their children and they lost contact with her after they moved to Texas where they continued teaching African Americans to read and write. God, was primary in their lives, speaking in tongues, worshiping God was a mainstay in their lives. God, kept them "covered by the blood of the lamb" so that they did not suffer from lynching which was a real possibility when they were living in Mississippi. Their perspective on life was to give "God the Glory and the Honor and the praise" and he will keep you all the days of your life.

Giving God the Glory, praising God, is very charismatic. Anyone can plug into the source, and receive the ability to speak in tongues, some people also can receive the ability to heal and be healed. My great, great grandparents held church in their home and they passed that down to their children. My great, grand mother Isabel Johnson, grandmother and grandpa Higgin's daughter, also held church in her home, and it was at one of these church services that I was "saved and filled" with the holy ghost and healed of chronic asthma.

My grandmother's mother Isabel Johnson was a very spiritual woman, she would walk around singing, and I've got, the "Joy, Joy, Joy, Joy, deep in my heart." I believe that she had Alzheimer's when she died, she was 93, it was with regret that my grandmother had to place her in a Convelesant hospital, and this directly contributed to her death. I worked in Convelesant hospitals right out of high school, and I was eye witness to abuse.

My great grandmother outlived three husbands, and she was a strict disciplinarian. At one point in time we had five living generations, with the birth of my daughter, she was the first of the fifth generation and Isabel Johnson lived to see that day. Mother Dear, as A.K.A. Isabel Johnson loved to have church at home.

As I watched everyone at this church service dancing around the room to gospel music, praising the lord and having a wonderful time, I wanted to feel what they felt, to experience the joy that the adults were experiencing. Everyone had lost their inhibitions, the music was playing, people were singing and dancing, and before I knew it, I was caught up in the spirit and I was dancing in the spirit of the lord also.

You absolutely know what you are doing, but it is more than you. Your heart is filled with so much love and joy that you can barely contain the love that you feel. You feel very light, and what ever problems you had are lifted. I continued in the spirit dancing and before I knew it I was speaking in tongues praising the lord. The joy I felt is difficult to describe, but you know that you are tapping into the source of all power.

Therefore many aspects of metaphysics are easily incorporated into my lifestyle. Many events which occurred in my life influenced the choices I made that either enhanced my spirituality or was a detriment to it, but I was conscious that my choices were going to bring be closer to my goal, which is to become one with God or pull me away from God. Sometimes events occur in your life and though you know better, you make a poor choice anyway. My mother Vivian Washington-Arthur lectured on "Making Choices, Paying Prices, and Reaping Rewards, which is something that each and every one of us does on a daily basis.

Chapter 20

A Debt to Pay

My mother's younger sister Sally is a prime example of this scenario. Sally was spirit filled, (meaning she believed in the holy ghost, shouted and spoke in tongues) with the best of them. Unfortunately Sally's life was not as happy as (from my perspective), it should have been. She died early in life because she put up with too much stuff from her husband, perceiving that she was doing the will of God. But there is only so much "crap" that the human spirit can take before it begins to affect you physically. My aunt thought she could handle the infidelity, until after many years she was hospitalized because she was spitting up blood. (It can be perceived as the spiritual ingestion of crap with a physical out come because it harms the mind body and soul) It was a direct result of the years of mental abuse that she had dealt with by trying to keep her family together. (God will not blame you for leaving an abusive spouse) When Sally passed the entire family knew that her life had been cut short because she had put up with too much mental abuse.

Her husband, before he passed knew he had a debt to pay. He (it was reported by his daughter while he was on his death bed), would not close his eyes because he was afraid to sleep. My cousin said she would hear him in the room after she had gone out arguing saying "I'm not going" he would sleep with his eyes open because he was afraid to die, because he knew how badly he had treated his wife, and he also realized that she was a child of God and lived right to the best of her ability. She walked the walk and talked the talk even though her husband did not reciprocate.

Of course Sally's death was a sad event for family members and friends alike, during this period John Friends, Sally's Step father, my grandmother's second husband also passed. Sally and John Friends were born on the same day in September and died close together. John Friends was a very nice man, spiritual and would give you the shirt off of his back. He married my grandmother when she came to California from Texas with 9 children in town. He was a good step father and did what he could to take care of all of his step children. Today, you would be hard pressed to find a man who would marry a woman who had 9 children that he would be responsible for taking care of. The question that begs to be asked is how my grandmother found herself in Bakersfield California after having moved from Texas with no husband and 9 children. In response to this question, there was a love triangle: Bertha, David and Oriene

Chapter 21

The Love Triangle

Bertha Massey married at the age of 14 in Long Branch Texas. Her mother Isabel married into a land owning family so therefore they lived well and were considered part of the upper class in Texas. Bertha met and fell in love with David Schrock, and soon after began having children, one after another. She did not know how not to have sex without having children. Therefore when a city woman name Oriene became their neighbor, Bertha thought she was going to learn ways of preventing pregnancy and other sophisticated city ways of life. Oriene was married also but was not in-love with her husband. The two couples became close and would stay up all night play cards and dominos.

This worked well until one day Bertha, (Big Momma) caught David coming from Oriene's house when he was supposed to be at work at the Railroad Station. There were ultimatums given, the bottom line was that David was in love with Oriene and she was in love with him. Big Momma did not want to leave her husband, but he could not promise not to see Oriene and she could not sit by and let her husband which she loved dearly go see another woman. Big Momma told her husband David, "David, it's either me or her. I will not sit by and let you make a fool out of me by seeing Oriene." "I can't promise you Big Momma May, that I am not going to see Oriene anymore." Big Momma responded, "Well you leave me no choice, these chil'en and I will be out of here by the end of the week." "Well Big Momma May I can't let you do that, I would hate to have to shoot you to keep you and my kids here." Big Momma also had a pistol that she had placed it in her

155

apron pockets, after a short stand off, Big Momma considered the possible out come of the situation, her keeping her 9 children in the fore front of her mind, she replied, "Well you know David I was only joking." But Big Momma was not joking; she gathered up all 9 of her children and moved them to Fresno, where here brother lived, then to Bakersfield where she had no relatives. It was a struggle for Big Momma, but she was determined to keep all of her children together, therefore when social workers came to help with grocery, they suggested that she separate the children and place them in Foster Care. Big Momma said, "Absolutely not, I'm going to keep all my children together."

The children were brought up with a good work ethic, they picked cotton in the fields of Bakersfield, and all children were expected to help out in one way or another. Their work ethic helped them throughout their adult lives, my mother became a professor, my aunt Joe Ann became a High School Teacher, my aunt Janice became a registered nurse, my aunt Glenn became a professional artist, and the boys became involved in various jobs, such as handyman, Insurance salesman, and construction contractor. Even though my grandmother was a single parent raising 9 children for many years, church played a major role in my grandmother's life and the lives of her children. Although picking cotton was difficult work, so difficult that one of her children reportedly stated, "whip me so I can go pick cotton, I hate picking cotton," he received his spanking and went and picked cotton. Moreover, they had seen their father pulled away from their mother by her best friend, and the children all managed to become productive citizens. Life was hard, but they had God and each other. The children tried to understand what seemed illogical as children, their father and their mother's best friend became an item. The children did not believe this pairing was a forever combination, they had always hoped their parents would eventually get back together.

The irony Of David and Oriene's pairing is that once they were together they lived up to the vow "till death do us part." Oriene died one year before David died, however Big Momma (Big Momma) died eight months after David died. These thee people lived on earth during the same period, their bonds were so strong that they all died within a year and a half of Oriene's death. The bonds that they established in this life seem to have contributed to their departure from this existence all within a short time frame.

Chapter 22

Big Momma's Death

The family knew when Big Momma was about to pass because she was seeing strange people in the house. When I heard about this, I made an effort to go visit her because it indicated to me that the spirits were here to accompany her on her transition from this dimension to the next. My Aunt Janice who she lived with told me that she kept seeing these strange people that no one else could see, another aunt Glen told me that she was instructed to go "tell the people she was busy." Soon after this, Big Momma passed on.

I truly believe that you do not die by yourself. I believe that someone is sent to accompany you and help you cross that great divide to make the transition easy. It can be a deceased relative or friend, just someone that will help to make your crossing easier. I had long wondered about this, especially with the advent of 911, and I thought of all those souls dying at the same approximate time, it made me feel better to realize that they were not alone. Also, there is nothing to fear, we do not stop existing, and we continue to exist just in a different dimension. I believe those who have crossed over know exactly how we are doing, and we can talk to them if we wish in our minds. The first law of thermo dynamics energy never dies; it only changes shape and form.

Chapter 23

Our Initial Meeting

My second husband, which was a marriage that lasted all of four months, was another painful experience in my life. I have found that at times I give in easily to coercion, because I don't have the tools to stop the badgering from taking place. Stan O'Niel A.K.A. Benjamin Kareem, appeared from our initial meetings to be a nice man, however, he was not on the same educational level as I, that is not always necessary, however in this case I should not have married him because he was Muslim and his belief system was too different from mine.

He was not exactly like the last man I had married, Stan seemed as though he had his act together. However one of his relatives warned me that he had some serious baggage. "Girl everything Stan tells you is probably not the truth." She meant that he exaggerates his stories. Every time I would see Stan he would ask me to marry him, and I would say no. He would say "Why won't you marry me? I have a good job, and I'm enrolled in college." "I can't marry you because you are Muslim. I know a little of what the Black Muslims are about, and I am Christian so we would be unequally yoked, in Christianity it is a sin to marry someone who is not of the same religion." For over two months this badgering took place. He wore me down until finally I said yes, "Only under these circumstances, you have to understand that I will never be Muslim. I was born and raised a Christian. And unless God's voice boomed out of the heavens loud enough for all to hear and God said, "Vanda it is now time for you to change your religion from Christianity to the Nation of Islam, I'm not doing it." As I was speaking to him I began to get very agitated so I felt that my point had been made, under no circumstances was I ever going to become Muslim. We married in Vegas, 3 months into the marriage I co-signed for him a Mazda RX7, which he would not let me drive, he left me with the car note, and that was a struggle.

I noticed that after I got off of work, I would not go home, I would go get something to eat, anything not to go home. Then one day Stan brought me some of his religious literature. He told me to read it so I could understand his beliefs. I read it and I was appalled at what it was stating. This literature was awful, it was violent and I couldn't understand why he would want to be a part of an organization that espoused violence. One part really struck me as awful "We've got to kill the blue eyed devils." I was so disturbed by what I had read that I told my mother about it. To me this wasn't a religion that was going to make the world a better place, it would corrupt the youth and create chaos and violence.

Stan asked me what I thought about the literature, I told him "it was awful; it was some of the most violent religious literature that I have read." It was at this point, which was about four months into the marriage that he said "My teacher says that you have to join the Nation of Islam." "I thought we discussed this issue before, I told you unless God, in a loud booming voice thunders out of the heavens above, "Vanda it is time to change your religion, I am not doing it." "My Teacher says we have to get a divorce if you do not join the Nation." I said, "God has not told me to change my religion, this religion is not even close to my beliefs. I won't change my religion from Christianity to the nation of Islam! I was born a Christian, it is the core of my foundation, and I will not change for you or anyone else. If your teacher says you must divorce me, and then do what you have to do, I'm not going to change my spiritual beliefs for you. I cannot, nor will I even try to change to something that goes against all of my principles."

He slammed out of the door and said that he would return to pick up his clothes the following day. That argument had taken so much out of me, I leaned against the wall, I thought we had an understanding, apparently we didn't. I just leaned against the wall and sobbed, I thought I had really picked a decent partner, no drug problem, he worked, and was going to school, I couldn't understand what had gone wrong. I felt like such a failure as a woman, that I couldn't make my marriage work.

My mother happened to walk through the front door of my apartment, I was sobbing, she said, "What is it." I told her through my tears that Stan was leaving because I would not join the Nation of Islam. I also told her we discussed this issue before we married and he said he understood, my mother said "After you are married, that is the time when men think they can change you." "I told him there was no way that I would change my religion, I found nothing good about his religion for me!" My mother asked, "Do you love him?" "Not really, I like him O.K., but this is my second marriage and I couldn't make it work." I never saw Stan O'Niel A.K.A. Benjamin Kareem again as his wife, he did not divorce me, and so, I divorced him. I wish that I knew then what I know today, about my choices and the reason for them being inappropriate, this one is obvious.

Chapter 24

Synchronicities

However during my lifetime there have been many instances synchronicities, which were lessons that I was to learn. I have encountered at minimum four different men named Chris or a derivative there of. It was not as if I went out requesting to meet men named Chris, to the contrary, I was trying not to meet anyone named Chris. The first Chris that I met after Christopher died was a completely different type of man. We were completely incompatible because of his ethnicity.

The second Chris that I went out on a couple of dates with was also incompatible, because of his ethnicity.

The last Chris I dated, was a serious relationship, we were to get married, we were engaged but not in love. I had given up on the idea that I would ever fall in love again, and at this point I was willing to settle in order to have another child. I desperately wanted to have a son, and Chris had no children at all and also wanted a child. He was also in the military like Christopher; he was a very smart man. Unfortunately I did not find out about his bad habits until it was too late. However, I was able to call off the wedding, and recoup any cash expenditures that I previously had, but at least all was not lost, I did not marry him.

The very sad thing about this Chris was, just as was with the first, he was a victim of circumstances. Chris loved his son dearly, he looked just like him, but he began to drink too much after we split up. He had been to visit his son and brought him toys and spent the night at my mom's house because by this time I was in a long term relationship. He said he would be back in approximately three months, but he didn't. So when he didn't call or show up I began proceedings for child support. I had been very flexible with Chris, but no call, no letter; I decided that I couldn't be nice any longer.

It occurred to me that Chris was probably dead. Why, I don't know, except that the last time he saw his son he was so very happy. All he did was spend time with him and stare at him; I guess he was amazed at how similar they looked. When he left I knew that he would be back as soon as he could in order to see his son. Mind you this is the only biological child that he has on earth, so far as he told me. So when there was no word from him or anything, deep in my soul I felt that he had passed on.

My court date arrived and I thought, oh they must have found Chris, because for several weeks no one had seen him. As I waited inside the court I looked around to see if I could spy Chris sitting somewhere in the court. I did not see him any where. When the case was announced, I looked around the room to see if I could see Chris, I did not see him.

From the corner of my left eye I saw a woman hurrying toward where I sat, I had just raised my hand to be recognized as the plaintiff in the matter. But before the woman could reach me, the D.A.'s investigator stated, "Your Honor, we feel Mr. Chris Coad is dead." By that time the woman reached me from children's services, she wanted to prepare me for this, before the statement was made but she was too late. She apologized; I thought it was nice that she tried to reach me in time.

It was not as if Chris and I were together, we were not, but I did not wish him any ill will. I found out later, that he had drunk too much. This was a very sad case because he was a nice man. I just couldn't be with him, initially we had been set up on a blind date. I just happen to encounter men named Chris.

What I can say about Chris, is that I did my best but I couldn't be with someone who abused his body with drugs and alcohol. When you are young, you sometimes experiment with drugs, but as an adult, that has no place in my life; I am an example for my children, they do more of what you do than what you tell them to do. I tried to support him through his rehabilitation, but there comes a time when you have to say enough is enough. However, if I were truly in love with Chris I would not have ever left him, the only man that I was ever in love with was killed, and that was the first Chris A.K.A. Pretty Boy Floyd. At the time, I felt that this was probably one of the last people in the family to die and we had earned a reprieve from death, I wish that this were the case.

Chapter 25

Romeo & Juliet

The next major wave of people moving on, passing from this dimension to the next, this began with my sister's husband Decker, Engineer, very bright young man, the love of my sister's life. My sister waited until she was 39 to marry her soul mate, they were both Cancer, they had the type of Romance that one only reads about. When she married him, he told her that he had cancer and that he had been fighting it for sometime. It would go into remission then it would flare up, but my sister being the prayer warrior that she is felt would be able to do every thing that it states to do in the bible and bring him back into remission. (Her husband reportedly saw two male angels before he passed), that didn't work, he passed and she went into a major funk and became mad at God, my mother and the world. At Decker's funeral my mother went over to give my sister a hug my sister stated vehemently, "Don't touch me!" My son wrote a story about it which he received an A on in his English class. "*The Mean Witch and the Handsome Prince*". 11/2 years after Robert died, my grandfather died, he was born around the same time as Robert, he was also a Cancer, my sister attended my grandfather's funeral in Dallas Texas, and I did not.

Although my sister Gigi and I did not always get along well during the beginning of our lives, it was no fault of my sister's; my father played a direct role in our relationship. When my sister was three years old my father, employing techniques which he had learned in the military, would give my sister the belt from his pants and order her to spank me. He would laugh and make a game out of this exercise, it was not discipline because I would not have done anything wrong or improper, it was only for his enjoyment. My sister growing up with my mother and father's love became a pretty balanced person and with our church going spiritual background, she was also very spiritual.

After my sister and I became adults, there were two very distinct examples of how connected we had become even though my father had created a certain amount of animosity in our relationship. My sister loved to shop, and often we would go shopping together, I think her favorite store was J.C. Penny's, I could be mistaken, but I think it was Penny's. I remember one day going into Penny's with Gigi, we had just entered the store, and I stood in the isle and looked around. I was not moving at all; my sister looked at me and said, "If go down this isle, and make a left at the elevators, it will take you to the restroom."

I looked at Gigi, incredulously, I asked, "How did you know that I wanted to use the restroom? Was I wiggling? Was I moving in any way that would have indicated that I had to use the restroom?" "No, didn't you say that you had to use the restroom?" "I said no. I didn't say anything, I do have to use the restroom, I was just thinking, I wish that I knew where the rest room was, but I never said a word." We just laughed that one off, the next incident we laughed about even more.

During Christmas, the family always exchanges gifts, my sister and I always try to get our mother very nice gifts. Gigi generally picks the best gifts overall for everyone in the family, everybody in the family looked forward to receiving a gift from Gigi because her gifts were always very thoughtful, something just for you. My gifts on the other hand were always nice, but just nice. As a matter of fact, one of the cousins stated that she would miss Gigi' Christmas gifts because they were always just for you, and they made each individual who received a gift from her feel special and loved.

On Christmas four years ago, Gigi and I were both excited about our mother opening up our Christmas gifts. We would take our wrapped gift and place it in front of her so that she would open our gift first; this Christmas I happened to beat Gigi giving mom my gift first, sometimes I was first, sometimes I wasn't. Well, as my mother un-swrapped my gift to her my sister sat and watched in disbelief, she said, "I can't believe this, I can't believe this." My mother loved her glass perfume chest that I had given her, it was unique, something that was special. It had six small containers of cologne, sitting on separate shelves, which were staggered in a clear window box.

My sister could hardly contain her excitement to have our mother unwrap her gift. As she un-wrapped the gift from Gigi, everyone stared in amazement, as the gift-wrap was slowly and carefully removed, because my mother hates to tear the paper, everyone's eyes were fixed on the gift. All of a sudden my brother Aaron began to laugh, he had seen the gift first, I could not tell from my proximity what type of gift she had given to Mom. Therefore, I stood up and walked over to the lounge chair that my mother was sitting in, to get a clear view of the gift. I could not believe it either and neither could my mother, my sister and I had given my mother the exact same gift for Christmas. It truly was amazing, my sister and I looked at each other and began to giggle, because we didn't go Christmas shopping together, and we would never tell each other what we were going to get mom, because we each wanted to get her the best gift.

I guess that God was saying to us, that we were both the same in his eyes and our mother's eyes, this was a really fun Christmas, this was synchronicity in action, it truly was amazing, we both said that we would return the gift for something else, but she said that was O.K., if I remember correctly, but that was fun. My sister and I were very connected to one another but my sister and her husband had one of the deepest connections, they were soul mates.

Chapter 26

We Played Hopscotch One more Time

Decker my sister's husband, passed at the end of April; and my sister contracted bacterial spinal meningitis and passed in June a year and a half later, their souls were truly connected. My mother called me when she took my sister to the Hospital, she told me to go back to sleep because it was about 12:00 a.m. My mother and I were to take some students to the Getty in the morning; my mother said that she would call me if she needed me. In those hours between sleep and being awake, I dreamed my sister and I were playing some of our child hood games, like we did in Fort Riley Kansas. We played jacks and hopscotch, and step on a crack break your mother's back. In the midst of the game I was playing with my sister, I said I was no longer interested in playing step on a crack; break my mother's back because that game in my opinion was all about death. Then the phone rang and it was my mother calling saying that they had to resuscitate my sister. In that instant, because of my dream I felt that my sister was passing. Therefore when I received a phone call at approximately 4:00 Am July 30th, my heart immediately plummeted as my brain searched to determine, "who could it be now?"

I didn't answer the telephone; however I could determine from the gist of the responses that it was something extremely bad. I thought about my brother Aaron, wondering if he had been distraught enough over my sister's death to do something crazy like committing suicide. Or possibly he had been in a car accident, because at times of deep grief some people over indulge in drugs and alcohol, I thought possibly alcohol for Aaron, because I realize that he has a beer every now and then. He and Gigi were very close because she helped raise him as a young child, she was the built in babysitter for Aaron. There was only a six year difference between Aaron and Gigi, where there was a nine year difference between Aaron and myself.

Therefore, I was married and off to Oklahoma during Aaron's formative years; and when I returned Aaron was 12 years old, and we really didn't have a relationship, however he was very close to Gigi. Moreover, Gigi was more like a mentor to Aaron, she worked hard to help him become successful at whatever he tried. Which meant that he tried to become successful at becoming an artist, a football player, however he was too thin for football, no meat on his bones. He did well as an artist, he had been encouraged by teachers and family to submit work in the County Fair, and he always placed, 1st, 2nd, or 3rd place. Aaron also became very active in student government and became involved in painting a mural on the basket ball gym at his High School.

Chapter 27

The Scorpio Gemini Love Game

During this period of time, he fell in love with his high school sweetheart; Maria, who is a Scorpio, which I am also. My brother is a Gemini, as are most of the men in our family. I have found that either Scorpio's and Gemini love or hate each other, generally the feelings are very intense as is true with Maria and Aaron. My brothers' had always been told that if they got a girl pregnant, they would have to take care of the baby, and that is what Aaron did. His relationship with Maria was volatile, to the point where Maria called the police on my brother because he was holding onto some of her things. At the time, they were staying at my mother's house, when the police came over to investigate what was taking place; my mother was infuriated with Maria and also upset with Aaron. My mother informed Maria that "When police are called into a dispute, and the dispute is between an African American man and a Caucasian woman, there is often the tendency to arrest the man, take him off to jail and throw away the keys." "But he wouldn't give me back my stuff." "Let me know what he has of yours and I assure you, you will get it back." My mother was fuming, she stated, "How could Maria feel that it was O.k. to call the police on her son while living in her home?" She told Maria, "I want you to pack your bags and get out of my house, right now!" And that is what Maria did, of course this was not the end of the Maria and Aaron episode, they got back together and went on to have another baby, Nanette. The first child Nicole, was sweet, mild and meek, their second child Nanette was not. She was defiant, and she loved both of her parents dearly.

Aaron went on to Jr. College and then was accepted to U.C.S.B.'s History program, at the time, I was working on my Teaching Credential at UCSB. Aaron and Maria moved into Married Student Housing, they actually lived close by me at the time. Their volatile relationship became even more dramatic, attending a university can play havoc on even the strongest relationship, which theirs wasn't. Aaron would stay out late, studying at Carrow's restaurant, which is where he met Sophia his current wife; she waited tables during the graveyard shift. Sophia and Aaron became good friends; she would continue her education at UCLA and receive a Doctorate of Jurisprudence degree.

Maria and Aaron argued over his relationship with Sophia along with the fact that he would stay out late at night studying, therefore Nicole and Nanette knew that Aaron had a relationship with Sophia while he was attending UCSB. Maria accused Aaron of having an affair with Sophia, but Aaron swore that he wasn't having an affair with her. I even asked Aaron myself if he had a relationship with her while he was married, he said, "No." Therefore when Aaron and Maria divorced, Maria divorced Aaron in order to go back to one of her old boyfriends, along with the fact that she just didn't trust Aaron. Aaron offered to keep his daughters and take care of them, initially Maria agreed however, life is tough and she needed money she determined that she could live a little better if she kept her daughters herself. Aaron was the ultimate Mr. Mom, not just because he is my brother, but because he did a good job being a mother and a father to his daughters. He combed their hair, and also had them involved in softball and basketball while finishing up his Bachelor's degree, which is a feat.

The court had awarded the girls to their father, ultimately when Maria decided that she wanted the girls back, this was another court battle. When children watch their parents fight over them and become enemies, they often feel responsible for the animosity between their parents, which is not the truth. Maria was awarded custody of the girls when she began having problems with the girls, so they asked to go back and live with Aaron again. This was an agreement made between Aaron and Maria, therefore during the last period of time between Nanette's living with Aaron and her death, Nanette had asked if she could move in with Aaron and Sophia; Aaron said no. There was bad blood between Nanette and Sophia; Nanette believed that Aaron had been unfaithful to her mother with Sophia while she was attending the University. Nanette cried during the entire wedding ceremony, all the guests and family members were very concerned about Nanette. I was very concerned about Nanette at Gigi's funeral, she was crying and crying, she stated "Now I have nobody." I told her that she had me also, and invited her to move in with me, she said that she would think about it. After she passed, one of her friends said that Nanette had come over my house to see me. I was sorry that I had not been home to talk to her. I believe that God in his mercy let Nanette come home because her soul and spirit had been too bruised while here on earth. Even if I had been able to talk Nanette out of suicide at that time, because of the bruises to her spirit and soul, she would have tried it at another point in time. She was my favorite niece; I was there when she was brought home from the hospital.

Nanette's death is directly connected to Gigi's death, my sister, one month after my sister, she took a gun and blew her brains out, and she was 16 years old. Nanette was caught up in a nasty divorce and other negative incidents, played a major factor in her untimely death. Nanette died on July 29, 2004.

Big Momma my grandmother was seeing and talking to spirits before she passed, she pulled the bandage off and bled to death she took both Gigi's and Nanette's death hard. (My grandmother died within one year of her first husband)

Chapter 28

Kenneth Jones And Vegas

After all the death and dying in the family, my mother and I decided to take a Trip to Las Vegas, my mother's favorite place. I came along to keep her company, I hate losing money in the slot machines. It is too hard to come by, and I never play enough to make any major winnings. Well Kenneth Jones,(I did not know his name at the time;) literally swept me off of my semi un-willing feet. I hoped in the back of my mind that I might me someone special, but I was definitely afraid to hope and definitely not on a Greyhound bus. First of all I hate ridding the Greyhound bus; my mother on the other hand loves ridding the bus. She is very gregarious and outgoing, I am not. It's not that I'm not friendly, it's just that half of the time I'm thinking about metaphysics and I don't want to interrupt my thought process. My mother and I made an agreement when we got on the bus in L.A. and that was, if the bus got crowded, because initially starting out there were plenty of seats, we would sit in separate seats however if the bus filled up we would give up our seats and sit together.

After leaving the L.A. bus station we stopped in North Hollywood to pick up more passengers. Well this ended up being a 15-20 minute layover because some passengers had missed the bus in L.A. As we sat there waiting for these 15 to 20 other passengers to get on the bus, my mom and I reiterated what we had previously stated, if there were too many passengers we would move to sit next to one another and let the passenger have our seat.

Can you imagine our surprise when one person boarded the bus. I saw him when he first stepped on board, I thought there must be some people behind him, I asked my mother, and "how many people can you see?" She was sitting on the right, I was on the left. She said "I don't see any other people." I asked, "Are you sure?" "Because if there are we can go ahead and move now." She said, "I don't see any other people." As the man boarded the bus my mother and I decided that the other passengers must be coming. As Kenneth moved closer to us, (we sat in the last few seats toward the back of the bus), I just knew he would stop and sit in one of the empty seats before he reached us in the back of the bus.

Kenneth, the young man in question is extremely good-looking African American man; when I saw him I thought he was drop dead gorgeous. I thought that I had grown past determine a person's eligibility by their looks; however I could not help appreciating a fine specimen of a man when I saw him. My heart raced, I have a tendency to do the opposite of what I really want to do at times. (Truly, truly I had hoped that he would sit next to me, deep down, but I also was afraid to hope that he would, because if he did what would I say to him and I was feeling a little shy and nervous, which is not something that I usually experience.) I know he will find a seat before he reaches me. I was ending a long term relationship and I was not trying to get involved, besides this trip was also to celebrate my birthday. My sister had really wanted us to stay at the Luxor, we cancelled the trip that we were supposed to have taken with my sister to Vegas in June because she died. So the trip that we were taking in November was to make up for the trip that we were unable to take with my sister.

Imagine my surprise when Kenneth sat down right next to me. (I did everything I knew to do to look uninterested, I looked out the window.) Perhaps he saw through my act? I was truly surprised when he said, "you don't mind if I sit here?" Now what am I supposed to say? How can I explain such conflicted emotions?

He was gorgeous, but, maybe too young, and I didn't feel like carrying on a conversation, there was so much to think about. I knew if he sat next to me the only thing that I would be thinking about was him.

My mother asked him when he got on the bus if he was someone special to make us wait for him. He said no, he was just a guy who had got caught up in a conversation and had missed the bus. My mother said, "Well I have never heard of the bus waiting for anyone. If you miss the bus, you are just out of luck."

Now back to my problem I really was not comfortable sitting next to Kenneth. Of course at the time I did not know what his name was. I looked across the Isle at my mother and I said, "Mom, get up, move, give him your seat and you can come and sit next to me."

Now at the time that I made this statement, Kenneth said, "What, you don't want to sit next to me?"

I didn't hear him say that, my mother told me afterward that he made that statement. Meanwhile, I am trying to get my mother to get up. So I said "Mom if you get up he will get up. I was basically pleading with my mother to move, she was probably thinking I was losing grip on reality."

I told Kenneth, "You get that entire seat to yourself you don't have to share with anyone. (I was totally intimidated by him and I did not feel like talking, too many deaths on my mind.) He was still reluctant, but he did eventually get up and move. He basically traded seats with my mother. My mother pulled him into conversation, she happened to have her book of poetry which she gave to him to read. She also gave him that copy of her book.

I on the other hand remained quiet initially. However, every now and then I felt comfortable enough to interject my thoughts. By the time we reached Barstow Station rest stop I was beginning to feel guilty about being so mean not wanting to sit next to him.

When we got off of the bus I went to my favorite area which housed the Egyptian artifacts. I purchased one or two, while coyly keeping my eyes peeled for Kenneth. I watched him go get food, when he returned I caught up to him and showed him my purchases, I asked him if he liked the Egyptian era. He said yes, I told him why we were going to Vegas and that after our first night we would be staying at the Luxor, on my birthday, explaining the significance of our trip. I took him over to the area where I had purchased my artifacts and left him there and headed back to the bus.

My mother was already on the bus by the time I arrived. However, for some reason, it was taking Kenneth a long time to return to the bus. The bus driver thought everyone was already on the bus and he was going to pull off, my mother shouted, wait, there is still someone not on the bus. Two minutes later Kenneth returned to the bus with a bag in his hand. He handed it to me and said "Happy Birthday." That was very kind. I felt really bad about the way I had acted. I said "Thank You" I opened the box, it was an Egyptian Artifact made of some type of turquoise that absorbs light. It was one of the nicest gifts that I received.

We traveled the rest of the way to Vegas, definitely getting along. When we arrived at the bus station we exchanged numbers, I gave Kenneth my cell and home phone number, and he gave my mother all of his information. We told him it was nice to have met him and we said our good byes. Well about 15-20 minutes after we got to our room Kenneth called and stated that his bus was not going to be leaving until morning and that he had no place to stay, although he has an Aunt that lives in Vegas her place was too small. I invited him to stay in our room on the floor, because my mother and I were sharing a room. He said O.K. he would come over. About an hour and a half later Kenneth arrived, we were eating. He came and joined us. Then he did something which was so totally sweet and surprising, he had the waiter bring a cup cake to the table with a candle in it and they sang me happy birthday. It was the best birthday ever.

We left the restaurant and went into the lobby, mom went to the room. Kenneth and I talked, and talked. I basically told him about my ex who I was still living with at the time but the relationship was over. I had given it too much time. And in talking to Kenneth and he to me, he told me about his ex we got close. We kissed; it was not just a smack on the mouth. It was a French kiss that struck a cord somewhere so deep in my soul that my heart raced, it moved the core of my being. We kissed and kissed, it was if our souls actually joined when we kissed. It was as if our souls floated somewhere out beyond the reach of humans and became intertwined to the extent that they were one and that was great. I told him I could feel him; our souls merged so completely that when I think about kissing him, I can still feel him. It is unreal that one person can move you so completely however if the basis of your analysis and assumptions are based on erroneous information, then your analysis of the situation, will be faulty. While Kenneth and I were Kissing, initially we began kissing sitting down in the lobby on a circular settee, then for some reason we stood, we only stopped kissing momentarily, and then, it was like magnets, our lips were caught up in another French kissing session, and as we kissed, there were many emotions going through my mind, body and soul. My mind was thinking, "wow" and smiling, if your mind can smile, and at the same time thinking, "what is this, it's so good, please don't stop, it feels so good." It was moving me from the bottom of my stomach, to the core of my heart. My toes were curling, as I stood there kissing Kenneth and I continued to think, "Oh my god, I don't even know this man, and look at how he can move, my soul." And then for some reason we began to move backwards. I paused momentarily to glance over my shoulder and see where we were headed. I thought to ask where we were headed, through our locked lips, he responded, to that wall, it is less crowded.

Believe it or not we did not break contact, we did not separate, and Kenneth gently backed me up until I felt the cold wall against my back. I had to smile through my passion locked lips; I had never done any thing like that before. But the emotions that I was feeling with Kenneth, were so, so, deep. I did not want him to stop kissing me; however we did have to stop kissing. I had noticed some rather unsavory looking characters in the Psalms. They were gathered in the lobby, it appeared as though there might be an argument at any minute. At some point during our embarrassing, my mother had come down to the gambling area which war right outside of the lobby. Kenneth was very quick, when he noticed that a fight might break out, he took me by the hand and we went in search of my mother. We found her at one of the one armed bandits gambling, and by then the ruckus had calmed down. So we headed off on our own, we walked to the restroom holding hands, Kenneth waited for me outside the restroom.

At the end of the evening, it was about 5:00 Am., Kenneth walked me back to my room and said good bye. It was a wonderful birthday; and therefore, I continue to hope and pray that we can find each other again someday, because I fell in love with him in 24 hours, I detached myself and tried not to feel my emotions for Kenneth, there was a lot of confusion, but when all is said and done, I still feel as deeply for him as I did when we met and it has almost been a year. I've talked with Kenneth but I haven't seen him. Only God knows how great my desire is to see him and be with him again. I try not to think about him because it hurts too badly. But when I am alone and no one else is around then the sadness hits me like a ton of bricks, then I cry for the love I lost. I would have never imagined that my heart would break over a man that I only spent 24 hours with, but the pain I feel for the loss is excruciating, my heart hurts so badly that at times I can only gasp for air through the waves of pain. And though I am letting myself feel the pain, I am holding back, because I don't want to cry too loudly, somebody might hear and then want to know what is wrong. I am truly broken hearted over the loss of this love, because there will never be another man like Kenneth.

At points during this past year, I thought that maybe there would be someone else out there who I could feel the deep intense emotional, spiritual and physical connection with, but no other man could reach that level of connection with me. Therefore I realize that meeting Kenneth was a blessing that God bestowed upon me, and blessings of this nature are rare. In my heart of hearts, I had fantasized about having children with Kenneth, I had even speculated on how they would look. But it appears that this was just a fantasy.

From time to time in one's life you have the opportunity to experience something that is so profound that completely changes your life in that it changes your perception of yourself. I have always thought that I was fairly grounded, evaluated situations and used deductive reasoning to come to logical conclusions however, I have found that the major, violent episodes in my life have created a person who has not made wise decisions, because my logic is based on faulty premises. There were times I felt I was in love, but upon further examination I have found that since my perception of what love is, was problematic it would be impossible in many instances for me to determine if I were in love or not.

Chapter 29

Choosing A Mate?

The realization came that although I use logic and deductive reasoning to choose a mate, through self-evaluation which entailed writing this book; it became very obvious to me that almost every man I had chosen to be with had issues similar to my father. It was not as if I went out looking for someone like my father, on the contrary. During this self evaluation analysis, it was obvious that my father really was a monster. I determined early in life that I did not like my father, and I was unaware until recently how his negative actions, impacted who I became. I became aware, during my father's funeral that I loved him, but I certainly did not like him.

There have been other times in my past when I have discovered that my thinking was problematic; generally it was in the midst of an event or an emotional occasion. Therefore while I was attending the University of California Summer Technological Institute for teachers in August of 2001, I had an epiphany, which occurred because upon analysis of historical documents I found I had trouble making elementary connections, which I had previously gained. I found that making connections that were obvious was giving me difficulty. So much so until I went to the Co-Director of the Institute Dr. Mary Baker and confided to her that I had a block. I termed it a block because I knew that I understood and should be making the connections, but there was something that I just could not get past. And I had no idea of what the block could have been.

Dr. Mary, listened intently and said very little, she was very sweet and supportive, but I did not think that she would follow it up, my hopes were that she understood the reason I was not doing a stellar job during the institute. Upon completion of the institute we had a dinner, during which time I told Dr. Mary and her husband that my fiancé and I were splitting up. Margaret and her husband mentioned that they knew someone that I might be interested in and he might also be interested in me, a man named Decker Snider. I said that was nice, but I never thought that it would come to fruition because we lived in different towns. Therefore my life continued, and I did not completely break up with my fiancé until 2003 when he moved to Hawaii, and I realized that I disassociated myself from difficult events.

Although, my disassociating was not something that I do which is well thought out, it is the realization that many childhood memories were not available to me it was an act of self preservation. I am cognizant of the fact that I do not want to remember the violent events therefore, when any events are strangely reminiscent of the past, I do whatever I can to stay away from pain. For example, my ex is an alcoholic, (not surprising) when he would become angry, he would try to pick an argument with me. I avoided arguing at all cost; I would walk out of the room to the bedroom, and go to bed. He would follow me raising his voice to continue the argument that I would not get pulled into. I would be very calm and I would quietly ask, "Why are you raising your voice? I am not raising my voice?" And that most often would take the wind out of his sails, but no matter what, I was completely detached, not feeling anything. The other thing that he would do, when I would try to detach was, go through the house, slamming all the cabinet doors in the kitchen. I would be in bed, listening to the doors being slammed, I was very afraid. He had never hit me but it scared me to death, I would put my head under the cover and a pillow on top of my head so that I would not hear the slamming of the doors.

I don't think my father slammed doors, but the violence of the slamming of those doors vaguely reminded me of something that I couldn't put my fingers on. And of course because he is an alcoholic he was very controlling, so he used his money to control me, through loaning me money to ensure that it would be difficult for me to leave him. Therefore I felt that I was incarcerated and his alcoholism made me very uncomfortable. Money Bags would drink 12-17 beers a night, every night.

With alcoholism, some like my ex like to use character assassination on their family members, however, I was unwilling to let him get away with using character assassination on myself or my son, character assassination was breaking the rules we had agreed upon on the onset of the relationship. I had detached so often in this relationship that there was no discomfort when the relationship was over, only relief.

As soon as this relationship was over I began to become active in my life's journey instead of passively coasting along the highways and byways of life. Therefore I decided that I would join a dating service, as a teacher I was always too busy to get out to a variety of places where I would encounter eligible men. I found the dating service to be interesting however somewhat time consuming. I was at the same time looking into matters of spirituality along with learning more about the horoscope.

Chapter 30

Hypnotherapy

I have always loved mysticism and spirituality especially when it deals with the growth and evolution of the soul. Therefore, I began to purchase books on journey of the soul. One book, struck me so profoundly that I actually wrote to the book's author. I was very interested in past life regression. I asked him if he would make an appointment with me to do past life regression because I had many experiences that would suggest that perhaps I had lived before.

The author Mr. Newman wrote me back and suggested someone else who could regress me because he no longer took clients. Although I was disappointed I was excited about the possibility of being regressed. The woman Ms. Nicole Smith, lived in Bianca California. I discovered Bianca California was up North, I made an appointment with Ms. Ritter to get regressed to get regressed. This was a very exciting notion for me, and I could barely wait to get there and go through regression. I enlisted my mother to drive to Bianca which was past San Jose.

The regression experience was very interesting; I was surprised by what came out of the regression. I stated that I had lived several previous lives, France, Amazon and in Egypt. I was not surprised about France, or Egypt, but I was surprised about the Amazon.

Apparently in Egypt I stated that I was Nefertiti and I was married to Amenhotep IV/ Akhenaten. "Amenhotep IV changed his name somewhere between the fifth and seventh year of his rule." At around the same period of time Nefertiti was given a second name Neferneferauten, "the most beautiful one of Aten." While being regressed, I spoke of Akenaten, teaching our children in a class situation, he was teaching all subjects, from history, science, math and spirituality, it was in this setting that Meritaten and Akenaten became involved. Our daughter was eager to learn and also very eager to please her father, her questions about Aten, the sun God. Akenaten changed their religion from polytheistic to monotheistic; he believed that Aten created everything. Not everyone was pleased with the change in religion, however out of respect for Akenaten his subjects went along with his new religion. He was also the priest of the new religion and Nefertiti was the Priestess, as the leaders of the new religion they conducted religious ceremonies which included their family.

While Akenaten courted Nefertiti, he was very romantic; he would compose poetry for her, because he believed that he was the luckiest man on earth to have been blessed with the love of Nefertiti, the most beautiful woman who lived. Not only was she beautiful but she was also intelligent and could help him rule Egypt, they would be co-rulers. They found through their meditation that they were able to communicate with one another with out verbalizing the message, this occurred because they were spiritually aligned and walking the same path. Initially Nefertiti was amazed at her ability to pick up on messages that were sent to her from Akenaten, she was even more astounded that he was able to pick up on messages from her. Akenaten loved Nefertiti deeply and completely, and she loved Akenaten from the depths of her soul, and she instinctively knew that she would protect him with her life if it were required of her.

Their love was what poets would have written about if they had access to information on the manner in which they loved one another. It was not that no other man or woman tried to interfere with their love, because there were many who thought they could influence Nefertiti or Akenaten to fall for them however, their love was intricately woven through each of their souls. And because communication for them was done by alternate means rather than just speaking, each one knew when and if the other was pulling away from the other. The couple shared everything, there was no separation for them regarding, money, politics, or religion. They were each other's backbone and strength, it was known that there was no deeper love than the love shared between Akenaten and Nefertiti. Moreover, when Akenanten decided to change the countries religion, he knew that he could do it because he had Nefertiti's undying love and support. Nefertiti should have realized that the only woman who could come between her and Akenaten's love would be a woman who had both her and Akenaten's blood running through her veins.

The new religion was a radical departure from their polytheistic roots, Akenaten was very inspired by the concept of the sun god, he was able to make sense of development of the world. The connections that he made, helped many of his subjects make sense of the world around them, his biggest supporter was Nefertiti until her daughter replaced her because of her thirst for knowledge and desire for her father and of the intricate operations of the Atmen. Nefertiti was astonished when she felt the loss of Akenaten's love.

It began with her inability to communicate with him through their usual means. At first she did not think anything of it because she knew that he was spending the majority of time with their daughter, until she observed them together walking hand in hand and then on another occasion, Meritertan sat on the lounge while Akenaten lay on his back, they looked like two lovers mesmerized by one another.

Nefertiti realized that Meritaten would spend hours with her father discussing the Atmen, trying to understand and apply her knowledge and also supporting Akenaten in the majority of his theories. Meritaten was very excited about the prospect of becoming a Priestess of Atmen. However Nefertiti, never thought that her beloved daughter would come between her and the man she loved more that life, her husband, Meritaten's father Akenaten. The realization of what was taking place, made her fall to her knees and double over in pain because, the two people that she loved most in life were betraying her by falling in love with one another. Although Nefertiti realized that often who you fall in love with is not within your control she also realized that you can control whether you act upon your desires, and therefore she walked around with a heavy heart.

Akenaten told his family that they were specially blessed by Atmen, and that Atmen followed them wherever they went in order to protect and watch over them and they were to notice when Atmen was following them in order to take time and give thanks to Atmen for their protection. Nefertiti decided to use the methods that she had been taught as priestess, she prayed to Atmen that what appeared to be taking place between her husband and daughter were not happening. The only thing that Nefertiti was willing to do was pray and talk to her King, husband and perhaps he could shed some light on what was taking place, maybe she was mistaking, perhaps she was reading more into what she saw than in actuality was taking place.

Akenaten's response was, "my Queen wife, who is any better for me to love than my daughter, who has your blood and my blood running through her veins. There is no one better. Though you are even more beautiful than you were when we married, our daughter is young, and in her youth there is an exuberance that is catching. And even you must admit, her body, and mind is attractive."

I expected him to deny that he had taken our daughter, but he did not, he defended his choice as if there was no other woman that he could logically have beside our daughter. My mind rebelled; it refused to believe that my love was taking the daughter that I bore, the seed that he planted. I loved my daughter with all of my heart also; I knew that I could not discuss this with her because; neither she nor I had any other recourse. I also knew that she loved sleeping with her father, and there would be no way to change her mind.

I became very sad and despondent; I just withered away in seclusion, very lonely. During the reading while I was talking, I actually began to cry softly because I knew that spiritually I had not evolved and I kept repeating that I didn't do a good job this life time. I was very sad, not crying loudly, just very despondent about the events of that life.

Upon completion of the reading Nicole asked me if I knew anything about Egyptian men having sex with their daughters. I said no, because I knew nothing at all about it. I had never read anything about it, but as soon as I returned home, I researched sex within the Egyptian family structure and found that yes, they did commit incest and often. I read about a case of a mommy of a 4 year old pregnant girl who was entombed with her fetus. Which of course today would not be possible, and it was surprising that it was possible during this period of time, today girls do not menstruate until they are eleven or twelve years old.

I had always been interested in Egyptian history, I had even arranged a trip for some of my students to Egypt, and I backed out for fear of hostilities toward Americans.

When I left Nicole house, I told her that I had an interesting regression and that someone should make a movie out of what I had experienced, she agreed with me.

I continued my search for enlightening books; I had begun writing a book of my own in 1998 which included some of the mystical experiences that I had encountered over my lifetime. During this period of time, I was looking for a perspective partner on the internet; I felt that somehow in someway I would encounter my soul mate.

One day when I was on the dating service I received a picture and an email from a man who had a catchy introduction. "How could a man like me get a woman like you to respond to his email?" I thought that it was very cute, but I waited for several days before I responded, he reminded me of someone, and I was just not sure who it was that he reminded me of. But, I loved the way he looked. He was sitting at a desk on a boat, the wood mahogany or oak, beautiful. He looked very comfortable at the desk on the boat. As I looked at him, I felt that I somehow knew him, but I didn't know how. It was April 28th when we first began to communicate with each other, and I found during our communications that I had finally found my Twin Flame, walking the same path in the evolution of our souls.

It is so wonderful and exciting to encounter someone closely aligned with the same type of spiritual beliefs that I possess. Our initial communications were regarding spirituality and mysticism. I had recently purchased a book on the Kabbalah. I had heard the term Kabbalah but I really didn't know what it meant, so as fate would have it, Decker Snider walked into my life just in time to help me understand what the term Kabbalah meant. Elizabeth Clare Prophet the author of the book that I purchased does an excellent job describing different aspects of Kabbalah however it is always helpful to me when there is someone I can ask questions.

After several weeks of communicating via the internet, Decker and I set a date to meet during the end of April, 2005. Where Decker and I are concerned there were many incidents of synchronicity that took during this period of time and continue today. When Decker called me to indicate that he had arrived in Oxnard, I was in deep deliberations about how I would tell him that I had M.S. It just so happened that when he called, I needed to pick up some paperwork from my doctor's office and I wanted to put off the meeting for an hour until I could return from the doctor's office. Decker was kind enough to offer to take me and this was fortuitous because the reason for my visit came out very easily.

Before I met Decker, I was very excited. I had butterflies in my stomach, I guess the usual jitters when you are about to meet someone new. I felt that he was going to be someone very important in my life, how or why, I wasn't sure at the time, I just knew that everything that had transpired before we met indicated that we were deeply connected.

When I saw Decker, I loved his appearance, his smile was heartwarming and invigorating, it made me feel as though I needed to be close to him. I looked into his blue eyes and thought, I know him from somewhere, I just couldn't place where I knew him from. I was so excited, that I knew that I was either going to repeat myself or stammer. I knew that he was going to be someone very special to me. It was as if I knew in my soul that my search for my love had somehow suddenly come to an end, even though I had no idea why I felt this way, only that I knew I never wanted him to leave my life.

Decker's persona embodies kindness, gentleness, intelligence and strength. He was very comfortable to be with and he was fun, he also has a good since of humor. We got along very well, there were no disagreements, and there was respect for each other's opinion. We really got along very well, we have the same interests and it was easy to agree upon our course of action for the day.

We went to a restaurant on the ocean, and after we were seated, Decker asked me to marry him. The first time he asked, I heard him but I didn't acknowledge it because I thought he must be joking. However he asked me again and I said yes. I said yes because I felt that I knew him, also I felt that he somehow knew me, which is what I told my mother. I called my mother while we were at the restaurant so that she could come and meet Decker.

When my mother arrived, she looked at Decker and said "He looks like Opa." And I said, "I knew that he looked like someone I knew, I just couldn't put my finger on who. My mother reiterated that Decker looked like Opa. Opa & Oma was the German family we lived with in Germany when I was two years old. And because of the entire trauma I suffered while in Germany Opa, was a comfort to me because he and Oma reflected peace and security.

With this beginning I thought that Decker and I were on our way to a great relationship, (great being seeing each other often), however this was not the case. I saw Decker once more in Oxnard, he attended our family's Mother's Day Brunch. He fit in very nicely with the rest of my family, it was there that he met my brothers and their families. Decker surprised me by picking up the tab for brunch, I thought that was sweet and we all enjoyed ourselves at brunch, and then he flew out of town on business. I had invited Decker to my brother's surprise birthday party in San Diego before he went out of town on business and Decker flew back just to attend the birthday party. It meant a lot to me that he returned to be with my family and I on my brother's birthday. Not only did he return for the Party, but he drove from L.A. to Oxnard and picked us up and drove us to the Party in San Diego, and drove us back to Oxnard the following day and returned to L.A. to catch a flight out for business, which indicated to me that he cares about me. Decker and I spent the night at a hotel in San Diego because my brother and sister-in law had a lot of company.

The following morning the hotel served a continental breakfast, and Decker was such a sweetheart. He treated me better than any man ever has, he wanted to make sure that I had everything that I needed, I felt treasured, he was so kind. I want to cry remembering how well he treated me. By the time we left San Diego we knew that we had a significant connection.

When Decker drove back to L.A., I felt sure that I would see him soon, but that was not to be. Decker knew what my family had known for some time, that I had some issues that I had neglected to deal with, which I was un aware of its complexity. Before I delve into this next section I must say this, which I will say again later, Decker sacrificed more than I know, and I know of some of the sacrifices in order to help me become complete. He has sacrificed not asking anything in return to help me resolve issues dealing with early childhood trauma, and family deaths.

Remember several pages back, while I was attending the Summer Technological Institute at U.C.S.B., Dr. Mary Baker and her husband had stated that they were going to introduce me to someone, Decker Snider? Well initially I didn't remember that they had made this statement, and when I did, I was surprised that I had overlooked that small but very important detail, which is what this is about.

While on the internet service I became involved with reading Tarot cards, which I knew nothing about prior to getting involved with the dating service. I was given decks of cards and I had to read them and analyze their meaning and apply it to my life. Well one set of cards that I read indicated to me that Decker was not being honest, that either he had a wife or a mistress or both and I became very upset and ended my engagement to Decker.

I recently began to realize the extent to which my father made our lives a living hell; the reality of the situation is painful moreover encompasses those actions that served to demoralize me; because I watched as a helpless child during the violent episodes.

Before Decker took me on this journey of self-realization, I did not have a valid basis for determining if I was in love with someone or not. Thank you is not enough to indicate how much I appreciate what he has done for me. It is the best gift he could have given me; to help me see that I was not whole, especially since I had always felt that I was, I just could not put my finger on why I made the decisions I made, which had catastrophic outcomes.

Chapter 31

Epilog

Through this journey I have been motivated to research alcoholism, in order to understand the disease moreover; because I am the child of an alcoholic I purchased several books that lead children of alcoholics toward recovery. A Guide for Adult Children of Alcoholics, Herbert L. Gravitz, Julie D. Bowden and Adult Children of Abusive Parents, Bagson Farmer, M.A., M.E.C.C.

These books were insightful; A Guide for Adult Children of Alcoholics helped me to understand how the events that took place when I was two contributed to who I have become. The roles that children of alcoholics take on were accurate in terms of describing how I survived the violence that took place in our household. My mother likes to describe how I would wake up early in the morning and get myself dressed, and I would also get my little sister dressed. Claudia Black has labeled the roles that Adult children of alcoholics take on and I find that I can identify myself in all three roles. #1"The **Responsible one** is usually the first born," I was the first born.

My mother likes to state, that from the age of approximately one year old, I would not let my mother dress me, "I'll get my own self dressed." Claudia Black maintains that "This is the child that begins to pick up responsibilities left behind by a trail of alcoholism and co-alcoholism." Moreover this child "In the midst of chaos, I'll take care of it." "These children are mature and reliable beyond their years." I would take care of my younger sister as a child, and little brother, I would also help out by doing the grocery shopping, cooking dinner, also my name was placed on my mother's checkbook. I was a child who never got in trouble in school, I always followed the rules.

Black also describes the children of alcoholic parents by stating; "these children appear quite well adjusted on the outside, they did not seem to feel." I cannot entirely contradict this statement, however it is not that you don't feel, you disassociate yourself from painful events so that you won't break down or show your vulnerability/weakness in front of people. If it is something that absolutely must be examined, it has to be examined in private, if at all.

Black's #2, **Adjuster** is also another aspect of who I am. "In the midst of chaos, I'll ignore it", which is something that I do all of the time. I never realized why I reacted this way during chaotic episodes, or even when asked an uncomfortable question, but this is exactly what I do. Often times it is to keep from getting dragged into an argument, or an uncomfortable discussion which I do not feel like dealing with. Therefore I adjust or adapt by detaching. I have found that many memories from childhood are repressed.

Placaters, is the 3rd category that Black assigns Children of Alcoholics, they try to fix people's feelings which is what I try to do. Of course when you are small and you see your mother with a Black eye and a busted lip, you tell her "Mom you look beautiful, all the men are going to like you." Of course this type of behavior has carried into my adult life, I actually was the sponsor for the "Conflict Resolution class" it appeared as though this class was a perfect fit for me however it was not, the core of what was being taught was absolutely right for me, however given the fact that I had no desire to deal with a class, which I felt the curriculum was too lose, because of my control issues; I was not comfortable teaching the class. However it is important for me to help whenever possible to negotiate a peaceful resolution to conflict. Therefore, I try to help people to see the other side of the coin, there is something positive that can be found in many situations and at work, in the past when friends & students were having problems with significant others, I felt that I was the voice of reason that could point out the positive aspect of the situation, generally it worked.

Therefore, along with counseling, and my new found knowledge of myself, it will enable me to grow and become a complete and mentally stable individual, making viable choices, in doing so, creating a better future for myself and my love ones. God has played a major role in my life enabling me to work my way through all of the death and violence. If it had not been for my staunch belief in God and my knowledge through my relationship with God, I don't know what my destiny would have been. However, be that as it may, I became a full time teacher, although I did not like teaching, my mother was a professor and felt that I would make a good teacher also, however because of the violence in my early childhood, I hated confrontations. Being a High School teacher, there are often times when there is no getting away from some type of confrontation, no matter how much diplomacy is employed. I hated going to work every day in one of my teaching assignments, I actually dreaded it, but when you embed yourself with financial obligations it is difficult to get out of your profession.

Therefore, I continued working in this profession for eleven years, after eight of those years I was diagnosed with Multiple Sclerosis, where your immune system is actually attacking your body. I was so conflicted about teaching, the income it provided, and hating every minute of it, but I wouldn't quit and leave it in the hands of God. The conflict created the health issue; it along with stress and tension, which were not visible to me. This makes complete sense to me, because why wouldn't I find a way out of a job that I was so uncomfortable with. Now that I have come to my senses, through self introspection and the help of Decker, I know that it is totally with in my power to turn my life around, I am empowered to take control of my life, and work my way through my issues stemming from child hood, to become a very happy person, enjoying my profession and my family with the help of God.

By Vanda K. Johnson

Photograph by Elizabeth Photography

I wrote this poem and after writing it, I felt the need for a definition for "Old Soul", and though I have met old souls, I am not one myself. I was inspired to write this poem about a young man who is advanced on many levels, physically, emotionally, financially and spiritually, and to the extent of his spirituality, I am not sure, but from what I see, he is the real deal.:)

Definition: Encarta: Showing mental or physical characteristics sometimes associated with a long life.

Is he an Old Soul?

Is he an old soul?
Is he?
He says his name
Is eternal?
That is what he
Found himself to be.

His name is eternal.
Is it a name
Or is it a concept,
Can that name,
be placed on
A human being?

A form with knowledge
That surpasses
All of his years on earth,
His soul is infinite,
It touches truths,
That many only scratch
The surface of,

He has touched
The face of the source,
He has folded him into his embrace.

Infinity is forever.
As is eternal,
His love for man
Is infinite and eternal

All knowledge is
In his hands
Because he is called eternal
And communes with the source
Eternally

What other explanation could there be
For one so young who
Was
And is now
Here

He never forgot
His purpose

His name is forever
Which means eternal?
Before the dawn of time
Never beginning and
Never ending
Eternal

By Naola Davis
6/23/2011
"Old Soul" Inspired by Jonathan Budd.

Notes from The Past Haunt My Soul

Notes that vibrate
From the strings of the violin,
Capture my heart
And in surrounding me with
Notes that enter into
The crevices of my soul,
It captures a joy
So deep that words cannot convey.
The joy that this melody brings

I have heard this type
Of music before,
Eons ago,
My soul remembers,
that which my mind cannot.

Stirrings of distant memories
And forbidden love spring forth,
Flooding my heart with a joy
So deep it seems real,
But it is not,
It cannot have been,
It is a fleeting memory,
Of a love once past;
The music returns it to me,
to a love long gone.

How can feelings from
Long ago be **real?**
Why is it the melody
Transports me to a distant shore?

Or is it just my love,
For the melody that
Traps my soul.

It makes my heart dance
And race,
And there is a. knowledge
That no one conveyed.
From a distant past.

My soul does hunger
And thirst for the melodic
Sounds that bring me,
Such deep joy and happiness
Or is it the ancestors
Of the past?
Long ago these notes
Were played, long ago
The soul felt the love
The melody brought,

The vibration of the
Strings, can never be
forgotten by the soul.

The soul's memory is long
As the notes that float
from strings in the air.

Return me to a place
Once forgotten,
But the memory lingers there.
The era captured
by the heart and soul.

The chords of the violin
Whisper magical, mystical melodies
To my heart,
It excites my spirit
And soothes my soul.

My heart smiles as the
Transcendental sound waves
Are emitted from
The heavenly instrument
That God has created for man.

As long as these vibrations exist
So will the soul's memory exist,
The notes from the past
Haunt my soul.

By Naola Davis
9/10/2011
poem inspired by "The Shoemaker Brothers"

He is the Leader Of The Free World

He is the leader
Of the free world
There has never
Been one like him.

There have been
Other leaders,
But none like
This man,
He is the leader
Of the free world.

He is beautiful
Inside and out
He is an erudite.
Without being pretentious
Or smug.

His knowledge is
Thorough,
He makes his people
Proud that he
Is the leader of the
Free world.

Many advances have
Been gained since
He became leader
Of the free world.

The free world
Was suffering an
Economic crisis, an
Economic melt down.
Before he became leader
Of the free world.

People were losing their homes,
Right and left,
Because there was
no employment to be found.
Sub-prime loans were given,
Easy in, ballooned you're out.
And people lost their homes,
The avalanche also took their cars.

Cash for clunkers was
Economic deal to turn the
Economy around,
And help our environment,
In one feld swoop.

Insurance for the uninsurable,
Was another measure,
The leader like no other implemented,
Because the ones who needed insurance most,
Could not be insured.

The leader of the
Free world, a
Brother like no other,
Strong intelligent, and wise
Controlled the free world.

Being not white, nor black.
By Naola Davis
8-2011

Nathaniel Davis

Me, my mother, sister and brothers

Daddy Jim, my father's father

Momma Ruby, my father's mother

Aunt Augusta at 101 years old, my great, great Aunt

Mother Dear's Sister Aunt Aida

Deborah, Roxanne and Vera, New Mexico

Sally Schrock Daniels

Sandy and Sally Higgins Great, Great Grand parents

Odessa, Big Mom, Ola and Sally

Papa,(John Friends) Nathaniel Davis and Big
Momma, Bertha Massey, (Schrock)

Latrinka and Harold

Ola Washington (mom)

Mary, Ola, Odessa, Alton, Glen and Joe Ann

Brenda Latrinka Davis   Nathan Davis   Jaiden and Lilianaola Davis

Latrinka Williams   Malia Duneff

Naola

Courtney Upchurch, Corey Upchurch, Weldon
Washington and Ivonda Mitchell.

Natalie and Dad   Kadeem and Ivonda

My nieces, Audrey, Ashley & Haley   My nieces, Danielle and Chantelle

Alton's children

Ashley at 5 years

Ashley, Haley, Audrey, Naola and Lexington

Cousins

Dauntie, Royce and Louis

Iva and Auntie Joe

Julia Dixon my best friend since high school and Angela Mitchell

Mom, Naola and Shauna

My children

My Stepfather and Mom

About The Author Naola Davis

Retired teacher from Oxnard High School, she graduated from the University California Santa Barbara, she also studied and recieved her teaching credential at UCSB, additionally she taught African American Literature at Ventura Community college as a part time instructor. She resides in Oxnard California and is the mother of two children. She is also a TV producer for the local community station in Ventura County. Naola Davis is available for speaking on topics related to History, Women, Children and Spirituality. Contact information Naola.davis@gmail.com.

Certificate of Appreciation

presented to

Naola Davis

In recognition of your important contribution to the ongoing fight
against hatred and intolerance in America.

The name shown above will be added to
the Wall of Tolerance in Montgomery, Alabama,
to provide inspiration to all those who choose
to take a stand against hatred.

Thank you for taking a stand.

MORRIS DEES, FOUNDER
SOUTHERN POVERTY LAW CENTER

Printed in the United States
By Bookmasters